EM

TO

PARENT

SINGLE PARENTING:
THE GUYANA REALITY

Copyright © 2024 by Paul Newman Benjamin
All rights reserved

Dedicated to all the young single parents who are determined to fulfill their God-given responsibility of parenting.

It takes a village to raise a child and a community to keep the parents sane.
- Ratzinger E. E. Nwobodo

CONTENTS

ILLUSTRATIONS xii

ACKNOWLEDGEMENTS xiv

FOREWARD xv

PREFACE xvi

CHAPTER 1. INTRODUCTION 1

    Geographic and Demographic Descriptions 3

    Definition of Key Words and Terms Used in this Book 5

    The Professional Conceptual Framework of this Book 6

    Bowlby's Attachment Theory 7

    Skinner's Operant Conditioning Theory 9

    Bowen's Family Systems Theory 9

    Minuchin's Family Structure Theory 10

    Summary 10

CHAPTER 2. LITERATURE THAT EMBODIES THE FRAMEWORK NECESSARY FOR THE TRANSFORMATION OF YOUNG SINGLE PARENTS 12

    Child-Raising Challenges of Young Single Parents 13

    Theories 18

        Attachment Theory 18

Operant Conditioning Theory 19

Family Systems Theory 21

Family Structure Theory 22

Facilitating Competent Parenting Among Young Single Parents 23

Transformational Leadership Through Empowerment for Single Parents 24

Reflective Leadership 25

Shalom Leadership 26

Appreciative Inquiry Model 28

Theological Foundations 30

The Life of Hagar 31

The Life of Naomi 32

The Life of the Widow at Zarephath 33

Summary 33

CHAPTER 3. INVESTIGATING THE PARENTING SKILLS NEEDED TO EMPOWER YOUNG SINGLE PARENTS IN THEIR ROLE AS PARENTS 35

The Methodology 35

The Sampling Method Employed 36

Data-Gathering Methods 39

    One-on-one Interview 40

    Questions 41

    Focus Group Discussions... 42

Data Analysis 45

Evaluation 46

Ethical Considerations 48

The Transformational Strategy Employed........................ 48

The Format of the Seminar 49

    The First Session.. 50

    The Second Session 51

Interventions and Observations.. 51

Summary 53

CHAPTER 4. DISCOVERING THE REALITIES OF SINGLE PARENTING 55

Demographics of the Participants 55

Themes Emerging from Responses to the Interviews............ 57

    Theme 1: The close bond shared between parents and children 57

    Theme 2: Meeting the daily needs of my children 58

    Theme 3: Lack of parenting skills 60

Theme 4: Lack of family support 61

Theme 5: No co-parenting 61

Theme 6: Financial burden 63

Theme 7: Balancing personal development and parenting 64

Theme 8: Giving love and affection 65

Theme 9: Providing a safe and secure environment 67

Theme 10: Exercising patience 68

Theme 11: How to discipline your child 69

Theme 12: Spending quality time with your children 70

Theme 13: Manage your spending 71

Theme 14: Prioritizing my well-being 72

Theme 15: Improving communication skills 73

Theme 16: Multitasking 75

Theme 17: Have a "can do" attitude 76

Theme 18: Know your limitations 77

Theme 19: Ask for help 79

Theme 20: Celebrate the achievements in your parenting 80

Demographics of Participants in the Focus Group

Discussions 81

    Focus group #1 (FG#1) 81

    Focus group #2 (FG#2) 82

    Focus Group #3 (FG#3) 83

Themes Emerging from Responses to the Focus Group Discussions 84

    Theme 1: Becoming a parent 84

    Theme 2: The strong bond shared between parents and children 85

    Theme 3: Providing for the daily needs of the children 86

    Theme 4: Lack of family support 87

    Theme 5: No co-parenting 88

    Theme 6: The ability to administer care for your children 89

    Theme 7: Giving love and affection 90

    Theme 8: Spending quality time with your children 92

    Theme 9: The need for community and government support 93

    Theme 10: The collaboration of healthcare workers, social workers, and religious leaders 94

    Theme 11: Being a role model 94

Theme 12: Mentorship 95

Convergence of the Main Themes Emerging from the Interviews and Focus Group Discussions 96

    The close bond shared between parents and children 97

    Lack of family support 97

    No co-parenting 97

    Giving love and affection 98

    Spending quality time with your children 99

Answering the Primary Research Question 99

    From the Parental Level 99

    From the community/societal level 100

Answering the Supporting Research Question 102

    From an individual perspective 103

    From a community perspective 103

Results of the Transformational Strategy 104

    Description 104

Post–Seminar Feedback 108

    Question 1: What impacted you the most in this seminar? 108

    Question 2: What are some of the changes you experienced being a part of this seminar? 109

Question 3: What will you do differently from today? .110

Question 4: What was your overall impression of this seminar? 110

Summary 112

CHAPTER 5. RECOMMENDING WORKABLE SOLUTIONS FOR SINGLE PARENTING SUCCESS 114

Interpretation of the Results 114

Transformational Leadership Perspectives Explained 120

The Validity and Trustworthiness of the Study 121

Significance and Implications 122

Communication Strategies Discovered 123

Replicability of the Transformational Model Implemented .123

Recommendations 125

Conclusion 127

REFERENCE LIST 129

APPENDIX A. ONE-ON-ONE INTERVIEW QUESTIONS 139

APPENDIX B. FOCUS GROUP DISCUSSION QUESTIONS .140

APPENDIX C. HOLISTIC EMPOWERMENT PLAN 141

ILLUSTRATIONS

Figures

1. Diagram Illustrating the Appreciative Inquiry "4-D" Cycle 29
2. Gender of Participants 56
3. Similar Themes Emerged from the Interviews and Focus Group Discussions 96
4. Responses from 'Discover' Activity - Identify one area of your life for personal growth and development 106
5. Responses from 'Destiny' Activity - How do you see yourself in the next 1 to 3 years? 108

Tables

1. Age Range of All Study Participants 38
2. Gender of All Study Participants 38
3. Employment Status of all Study Participants 39
4. Demographics of Participants by Gender 55
5. Age Range of Participants 57
6. Employment Status of Participants 57
7. Participant Responses to Question 2: Describe some of the challenges you face as a single parent 59
8. Participant Responses to Question 4: Give an example of a challenge you faced as a single parent and how you addressed it 63
9. Participant Responses to Question 5: What are the most essential skills young single parents need? 66

10. Participant Responses to Question 6: If there is one experience you can share to help other young single parents in raising their children, what would it be and why? 73

11. Participant Responses to Question 7. What can you do to improve your parenting skills? 75

12. Participant Responses to Question 8. What can be done to make parenting easier for young single parents? 78

13. Participant Responses to Question 9. What recommendations will you give to help young single parents become more confident as parents? 81

14. The Age Range of Participants in Focus Group 1 82

15. The Age Range of Participants in Focus Group 2 82

16. Employment Status of Participants in Focus Group 2 83

17. Age Range of Participants in Focus Group 3 83

18. Employment Status of Participants in Focus Group 3 83

19. Peak Experiences in Your Parenting 84

20. Challenges You Face in Your Daily Child-raising Experiences 87

21. Most Essential Skills Young Single Parents Need to Help Them Become More Confident as Parents. 91

22. Responses from 'Dream' Activity - Identify an institution you would like to attend to achieve the goal of personal growth and development 107

xiii

ACKNOWLEDGEMENTS

I give thanks to Almighty God for giving me the strength and the knowledge to complete this book. He has truly been faithful.

To my dear wife Tracy, thank you for your words of encouragement and acts of kindness that motivated me to persevere. I am grateful to my immediate and extended family who enquired or visited to monitor my progress in this book. Your interventions were inspirational.

I give honor to Bishop Dr. Murtland Raphael Massiah CCH. As my bishop and mentor, you spoke into my life and encouraged me to pursue higher education. Special thanks to Mrs. Shevone Corbin and Mr. Anthony Foster who have diligently journeyed with me throughout the writing of this book.

Heartfelt gratitude is expressed to Dr. Marcel Hutson and Dr. Joy Wilson, Professors Bill Payne, Claire Henry, and Judi Melton from Bakke Graduate University for your invaluable contributions that were utilized in this book.

FOREWARD

Many books have been written on single parenting; however, this book, in particular, is unique in that it embodies a research component with real-life experiences in addressing the intricacies of the subject matter. It proves that resilience is the guiding light in the journey of single parenting. This book explores the challenges and triumphs, offering insights and support to those navigating the intricate path of raising a child solo. Through shared experiences and practical advice, Dr. Benjamin aims to empower single parents, fostering a sense of community in the face of unique trials.

Specifically, in the following chapters, Dr. Benjamin delves into the profound essence of single parenting by postulating various theories and practices. These theories and practices were carefully considered with a sound research methodology. He arrives at some of his conclusions through the lens of those who navigate the solitary path of raising children. This approach to the issue proved that love, compassion, strength, sacrifice, and unwavering determination are central to raising children solo.

These pages serve as a source of strength, encouragement, and a reminder that the single-parent journey, though challenging, is a testament to the extraordinary strength within every such parent and that, though it seems insurmountable, it is achievable.

Dr. Marcel Hutson, Professor of Servant Leadership, BGU

PREFACE

The purpose of this book is to promulgate the child-raising challenges young single parents face in their role as parents and to explore ways to help mitigate the challenges they face in parenting. I am of the firm belief that young single parents have great potential and have embraced opportunities that come within their reach, thus propelling them to move to another level in society.

This book has therefore responded to the challenges by presenting a collaborative approach among stakeholders which includes, parents, educators, faith-based and community leaders to mitigate those challenges and mobilize support to empower young single parents in their role as parents. A transformational intervention was used to establish some of the factors that contribute to the lack of parenting skills and address them systematically to facilitate the parenting of young single-parent families for improved and sustainable community development.

In this book I provided a forum for integral training through an empowerment seminar that will transform the parenting experiences of young single-parent fathers and mothers, empowering them with the requisite knowledge, leadership skills, and proactive attitudes to perform optimally in their role as parents. Through the Appreciate Inquiry (AI) approach and the employment of transformational leadership perspectives of reflective and shalom leadership, young single parents were inspired to engage in the process of personal growth and development. This approach provided a safe space for parents to share their experiences and co-create dreams for their families.

Given the fact that the challenges faced by single parents are a worldwide phenomenon, careful consideration was given to the audience of policymakers at the national and international level, such as the Gender Affairs Bureau of the Ministry of Human Services and Social Security, funding agencies such as UNICEF and UNDP as well as other research practitioners who can use the data to fund programs that will bring relief to people based on the problems they are experiencing in the community. The book has some key recommendations such as a holistic empowerment plan, that addresses social, financial, and educational skillsets required in parenting. The empowerment plan includes unique approaches such as organizing appropriate relationship counseling sessions to address matters of low self-esteem, anger management, emotional healing, and mental health well-being among young single parents. The integration of shalom leadership yielded gratifying responses from young single parents who expressed comfort in knowing that there were still persons and entities concerned by their situations and are willing to empower them to dream again for their families. There is an African Proverb that says, "If you want to go fast go alone, if you want to go far, go together."

My sincere hope is that the readers of this book will be inspired to join me in the noble cause of empowering young single parents to fulfill their God-given responsibility of parenting.

CHAPTER 1
INTRODUCTION

The single-parent family is a part of the main family types accepted in society today, consisting of one parent with one or more children. The Organization for Economic Cooperation and Development (2014, as cited in The Spaced-Out Scientist, 2017) states,

- 17% of children aged 0-14 live in single-parent households worldwide
- women head approximately 88% of these households
- contrary to popular belief, the majority of single parents are employed. (p. 1)

In my experiences of interacting with young single parents, I see evidence of brokenness, poverty, and the challenges they face in their daily lives. These realities have created a burden for me to investigate the signs of need and how I could be a part of transforming their situation.

Several studies have revealed the challenges single parents face in their role as parents. In one such study in England, Stack and Meredith (2018) highlighted the fact that "the stresses of parenting alone appear to heighten feelings of stress, uncertainty, and depression associated with finances" (p. 241). Henry (2017) in her study on Child Neglect in Guyana, discovered that "forty percent of reported cases of unsupervised children were due to the work of the parent or caregiver. Some single parents are security officers, or work in jobs requiring them to work at night or leave early in the morning" (p. 31).

In context to the family structure in the Caribbean, Ken (2007) in a study posited "The concept of a 'Family' being that of a mother, father and children are not a given in the Caribbean, especially in families of lower socioeconomic status" (p. 6). Ken also found that "where children were separated from parents, nearly all were single women supporting a household" (p. 6). According to Cordeiro (2022),

> The single-mother situation is not new or unique to Trinidad and Tobago. Yet its persistence and exacerbation are of great concern. There seems to be a generational cycle of single motherhood in the twin-island country, a pointer to simmering, underlying societal problems. Hence the need for sustainable transformation of society as a lasting solution with far-reaching effects on children's education from single-mother households. (p. 2)

Cordeiro (2022) has concluded that there should be efforts to curtail the vicious cycle of single motherhood through sustainable, transformative solutions. There is a need for a holistic approach that addresses the root causes of injustices that propagate lone motherhood. The studies mentioned have highlighted some of the challenges single parents face in Guyana, the Caribbean, and further afield. Based on the aforementioned, this book investigates the child-raising challenges of young single parents in 'C' Field Sophia, Georgetown, Guyana, and explore ways to help such parents mitigate the challenges they face in parenting.

Geographic and Demographic Descriptions

According to the Encyclopedia Britannica (2015),

Georgetown is the capital city of Guyana. The country's chief port, Georgetown lies on the Atlantic Ocean at the mouth of the Demerara River. Although the settlement was founded by the British in 1781 and named for King George III, it had been largely rebuilt by the French by 1784. Known during the Dutch occupation as Stabroek, it was established as the seat of government of the combined colonies of Essequibo and Demerara in 1784. (p. 1)

Its culture reflects the facets of Amerindian, East Indian, Chinese, African, Portuguese, and Europeans. These diverse origins of its people are celebrated on several holidays, such as Easter, Phagwah, Emancipation, and Christmas. Georgetown is known for its British colonial architecture- St George's Cathedral and its iconic Stabroek Market. The most important institutions of government and commerce include the executive departments, Parliament

Buildings, The Law Courts, the Central bank, and Commercial Banks. The city is a very diverse city with resilient hard-working people.

Sophia is a semi-urban community that has been developed over the past 30 years for low-income and middle-income housing and is located on the outskirts of the capital city. It was once a squatting area now becoming regularized. Because of the transition from squatter settlement, the community process of formalizing social infrastructures such as schools, health centers, community centers, churches, play fields, and such is ongoing.

According to the most recently published Guyana Population and Housing Census (2012) by the Bureau of Statistics of Guyana, 26% of the Sophia population received primary education; 59% received secondary education; 3% received post-secondary education, and 6% received a university education. In terms of economic activity, 55% of the population had a job and work, 2% sought a first job, 2% sought a job which was not the first, 11% attended school, 23% performed home duties, and 5% were retired or did not work.

The Community of Sophia has grown significantly since the last published population and housing census in 2012. Anecdotal evidence and personal observation suggest that the population has grown an estimated 200 percent because of its expansion since 2012.

Definition of Key Words and Terms Used in this Book

The term *single parent* "is simply that one parent raises a child in their household without a partner living with them" (Cook, 2021, p. 1).

Parenting skills refer to "the natural and accurate and specific ability, experience, knowledge, intuition, qualities, and skills to be an effective and loving parent to a baby, child, or children" (Mary, 2016, p. 1).

The term *attachment theory* "is a basic human need for a secure relationship between children and caregivers" (Ali & Soomar, 2019, p. 2).

The term *operant conditioning theory* "means changing behavior by providing reinforcement after desirable behavior" (Ali & Soomar, 2019, p. 2).

The term *family systems theory* "emphasizes the idea that families are continuous entities, with rules, beliefs, and values that shape members over time" (Pfieffer, 2021, p. 1).

The *family structure theory* refers to "structural family therapy as a type of family therapy that looks at the structure of a family unit and improves the interactions between family members" (Cherry, 2021, p. 1).

The Professional Conceptual Framework of this Book

Merriam (2009) states "A theoretical framework is the underlying structure, the scaffolding or frame of your study. Further, a theoretical framework underlies all research" (p. 66). It is, therefore, imperative that I state the following theoretical framework that undergirded the study in this book. They are as follows.

- Bowlby's attachment theory
- Skinner's operant conditioning theory
- Bowen's family systems theory
- Minuchin's family structure theory

Ainsworth and Bowlby (1991) proffer "Attachment theory is the joint work of John Bowlby and Mary Ainsworth" (p. 1). Bowlby's attachment theory applies to this study since it promotes the positive effects of bonding between a parent and a child/children. The authors continue to say,

> Bowlby's major conclusion, grounded in the available empirical evidence, was that to grow up mentally healthy, the infant and young child should experience a warm, intimate, and continuous relationship with his mother (or permanent mother substitute) in which both find satisfaction and enjoyment. (p. 7)

Bowlby's attachment theory is significant in developing effective parenting skills for single parents. The practice of effective parenting skills will motivate parents to repeat behaviors that create favorable results for their children's well-being and can influence most aspects of learning and child development. Cherry (2023) states,

> Operant conditioning, sometimes referred to as instrumental conditioning, is a method of learning that employs rewards and punishments for behavior. Through operant conditioning, an association is made between a behavior and a consequence (whether negative or positive) for that behavior. (p. 1)

The Regain Editorial Team (2023) explained that in the Bowen family system theory "Family impacts one another to some extent, and what happens to one will positively or negatively impact others, affecting their thoughts, feelings, and behaviors" (p. 1).

Further, UKessays (2015b) writes "The structural theory sees the family as an integrated whole. Therefore, the emphasis should be on contextual problems and solutions rather than an individual" (p. 1). The aforementioned theories will certainly help in the process of empowering the single-parent family.

Bowlby's Attachment Theory

Cherry (2022) states,

Attachment is an emotional bond with another person. Bowlby believed that the earliest bonds formed by children with their caregivers have a tremendous impact that continues throughout life. He suggested that attachment also serves to keep the infant close to the mother, thus improving the child's chances of survival. (p. 2)

This view of attachment was shared by both male and female participants of my study as a high point in their parenting. Cherry (2022) continues to say,

Throughout history, children who maintained proximity to an attachment figure were more likely to receive comfort and protection, and therefore more likely to survive adulthood. Through the process of natural selection, a motivational system designed to regulate attachment emerged. (p. 2)

In my view, the process of attachment is critical for the positive outcomes that parents desire for their children. Further, children will feel safe and cared for and more confident in their daily decision-making. The lack of attachment may result in some children having behavioral challenges as they grow in life.

The application of attachment theory in developing effective parenting skills for single parents was of significance in this study. The parent-child relationship has a major influence on most aspects of child development. Optimal parenting skills and behaviors have a positive impact on children's self-esteem.

Skinner's Operant Conditioning Theory

McLeod (2023) states "Operant Conditioning, also known as instrumental conditioning, is a method of learning normally attributed to B.F Skinner, where the consequences of a response determine the probability of it being repeated" (p. 1). McLeod further stated, "Through operant conditioning behavior which is reinforced (rewarded) will likely be repeated, and behavior which is punished will occur less frequently" (p. 1). Skinner believed the best way to understand behavior is to look at the causes of an action and its consequences. Operant conditioning involves learning through the consequences of behavior.

Bowen's Family Systems Theory

Regain Editorial Team (2023) states,

Dr. Murray Bowen developed the Bowen family systems theory (Bowen theory). One of the central premises behind the Bowen family systems theory is that families and the people in them function as one emotional system, which means it may be easier to understand people by viewing them in the context of their family relationships. This theory suggests that understanding someone's family story can help understand how they think, feel, and behave. Family impacts one another to some extent, and what happens to one will positively or negatively impact others, affecting their thoughts, feelings, and behaviors. (p. 1)

Regain Editorial Team goes on to say that "Family relationships are very complex, and no two families are alike. However, the family systems theory suggests that each family is one big emotional system and that each part of the family unit affects everyone else" (p. 1).

Minuchin's Family Structure Theory

UK Essays (2015b) states "The structure of the family provides an understanding of the patterns that develop over time within a family allow it to maintain stable while existing in a changing environment" (p. 2). UK Essays further states "The structural theory sees the family as an integrated whole. Therefore, the emphasis should be on contextual problems and solutions rather than an individual" (p. 1). It focuses on family interactions to understand the structure or organization of the family. Goldenberg and Goldenberg (as cited in UK Essays (2015b) stressed "The family structure represents the operational rules that govern the way family members interact with each other" (p. 1).

Summary

Addressing the parenting skills needed for young single parents to empower them in their role as parents in 'C' Field Sophia,

Georgetown, Guyana was of paramount importance. This is so because it allowed parents to share personal beliefs and values with their children while they learned what concerns and priorities they have. Therefore, the professional conceptual framework used to guide this process was John Bowlby's attachment theory, B.F. Skinner's Operant conditioning theory, Bowen's Family systems theory, and Minuchin's Family structure theory. These theories provided an opportunity for parents to practice effective parenting skills and motivated them to repeat behaviors that created favorable results in their children's well-being. This approach helps to influence most aspects of learning and child development.

    The following chapter will review the literature on the following concepts of child-raising challenges of young single parents, Bowlby's attachment theory, Skinner's operant conditioning theory, Bowen's family system theory, and Minuchin's family structure theory.

CHAPTER 2
LITERATURE THAT EMBODIES THE FRAMEWORK NECESSARY FOR THE TRANSFORMATION OF YOUNG SINGLE PARENTS

Meriam and Tisdell (2016) explained "One function of the literature review is to provide the foundation for contributing to the knowledge base" (p. 90). Meriam and Tisdell further submit "A commanding knowledge of previous studies and writing on a topic offers a point of reference for discussing the contribution the current study will make to advancing the knowledge base in this area" (p. 91). I was not able to find an array of literature on the subject matter in my home country. The literature review is organized into the following sections.

1. Child-Raising Challenges of Young Single Parents
2. John Bowlby Attachment Theory
3. B.F. Skinner Operant Conditioning Theory
4. Bowen Family Systems Theory
5. Minuchin Family Structure Theory
6. Facilitating Competent Parenting Among Young Single Parents
7. Transformational Leadership Through Empowerment for Single Parents
8. BGU's Transformational Leadership Perspectives

9. Appreciative Inquiry Model

10. Theological Foundations

11. Investigating the Life of Single Parents in the Bible

Although the theories studied highlighted Western culture, they apply to the Guyanese context. Single parents in the culture of the West and the Guyanese context are faced with similar challenges of earning, poverty, and raising children. Better Health Channel (2022) states "Single parents may experience the challenges of attempting to fulfill the role of 2 parents as a sole person and income earner. Many can feel burnt out by this task, as it is unrealistic and stressful" (p. 2).

Child-Raising Challenges of Young Single Parents

Researchers have indicated that there are child-raising challenges faced by single parents in their role as parents. In one such study, Bhat and Patil (2019) state "Single parenting is a social sacrifice and unpleasant test of stamina in one's life for bringing up the child" (p. 161). The authors also say that one reason for single parenting in India is 'Marriage against the wish.' Sometimes parents of Indian children forcefully want to marry their children against their wishes and choices which often results in single parenting. Bhat and Patil have concluded that "single parents are forced to work to support the household expenses, lifestyle maintenance, and future planning requirement. For the single parent, there is little time for normal household work in addition to earning and living and raising children" (p. 164). Their study also states "The family environment includes the behavior created within a family and develops a child's personality. The effective family functioning in conditioning the children's personality and social development has outstanding importance" (p. 162). Therefore, I posit that my study examined the family systems theory and Minuchin's family structure theory and highlighted how it promoted cooperation among family members and strengthened family systems in empowering single parents in their role as parents.

Nwobodo (2021) proffers,

This study in its exposition reveals that regardless of culture, poverty has a significant impact on the parental practices adopted by parents. In other words, poverty stands as a serious barrier to proper parenting hence, speedy effort should be made to alleviate poverty as well as teach parents good parental practices for the best outcome of the child. (p. 65)

Nwobodo (2021) also states,

There is evidence from research in the area of parenting that poverty plays a critical role in the parenting attitudes and styles and practices of low-income parents. However, researchers have no consensus on whether or not poverty affects parenting. Dermott and

Pomati (2016) argue that "poor parents are not always poor at parenting." (p. 66)

The study adds to the body of literature on poverty and parenting. The "findings also show that poverty affects the moral development of the child" (Nwobodo, 2021, p. 75). Further, "Poverty poses a serious challenge to the primary duties of parents and proper parenting" (p. 75). Nwobodo recommended that "the church and other religious bodies should as well develop parenting goal-driven courses that will equip intending couples with the skill and knowledge of parenting" (p. 75). Based on this premise, my study embraced a collaborative approach with the community, the health center, the churches, and the nursery school. While Nwobodo (2021) exposed how poverty compromises parenting regardless of ethnicity and culture, it underscores the need to facilitate parents in their role as parents. It becomes expedient to chart a way forward to enhance proper parenting.

Oshi et al. (2018) examined the potential relationship between Jamaican secondary students' alcohol drinking habits and their family structure. The results revealed that "out of 3,365 students, 1,044 (31.0%) were from single-parent families. However, family structure was not significantly associated with the past year and past month alcohol use" (p. 19). The study concluded that family structure is an independent predictor of alcohol use among high school students in Jamaica. The authors used material, methods, and data from a nationally representative sample and the National Secondary School Survey. Regarding these data sources, the authors say "The National Secondary School Survey received approval from the Jamaican Ministry of Health as well as the Ethics Committee of the Faculty of Medical Sciences of the University of the West Indies Mona, Campus" (p. 20). The study concluded that it may be useful to conduct further research to ascertain the reasons for this outcome. This study investigated the areas in which single parents may need help with parenting from an appreciative inquiry approach. A key factor in building a positive parent-child relationship is for children to have nurturing, warm, sensitive, responsive, and flexible parenting.

Radford (2021) announced,

> The University of the West Indies (UWI) Open Campus and the Jamaica Alumnae Chapter (JAC) of Delta Sigma Thea Sorority, Incorporated, announced a partnership that will support students who are single mothers, as well as programs to strengthen the professional development of alumna and advancing students. (p. 1)

Radford (2021) further proffers "The partnership seeks to support the primary demographic of UWI Open Campus students who are single mothers striving to complete their online education, while often working in the tourism and business process outsourcing industries" (p. 1). The partnership is a step in the right direction, and my study sought to emulate this plan of action for single parents in the 'C' Field Sophia community. This plan of action is emergent and was addressed at the destiny phase of the 4-D cycle approach of AI in the empowerment seminar held as part of the transformational strategy in my study.

> The United Nations Sustainable Development Group (2021) stated the following. Single mothers have had a hard time of it during the pandemic. They may often face a choice between caring for their children and earning money to support them. With their children's in-person classes cancelled, mothers face added pressure of supervising online classes. Jobs – already hard to find – have evaporated across the economy. Now, many single mothers are worried if they can ever dig themselves out, or if the struggle will have lasting consequences for their children's happiness. Dozens of low-skilled single mothers with infants can now breathe a little easier, as the UN and the Government of Saint Lucia have teamed up to help them weather the current crisis and get them better equipped for life after COVID-19. (p. 1)

Single mothers in 'C' Field, Sophia, are faced with similar challenges highlighted in this article. My study explored some of these challenges and sought ways to facilitate single parents in their role as parents.

Theories

Attachment Theory

Attachment theory is ascribed to John Bowlby as the originator. Ali and Soomar (2019) comment on the fact that "Parents facilitate their children in each step of their life and love them unconditionally" (p. 1). This submission is a critical parenting skill that is needed for young single parents in the rearing and caring of their children. This practice will help to build strong and lasting relationships between parents and children. "However, as a result of single parenting, this love, and warm-heartedness seemed to decrease that directly affect the child's overall health status and upbringing" (p. 1).

Ali and Soomar (2019) further submit,

> Attachment is a basic human need for a secure relationship between children and caregivers. A child psychiatrist John Bowlby gave the theory of attachment which clearly explains how children and parent relationship emerges and how it influences the emotional and social development of a child. Four stages of attachment were designed by Bowlby. These stages begin from infancy. These stages are pre-

attachment, attachment in making, clear-cut attachment, and formation of a reciprocal relationship. (p. 2)

Ali and Soomar (2019) have concluded and recommended that "Despite only stigmatizing single parents and their children, we all as a community should help them in fulfilling their requirements or needs to make their life valuable and provide them with a platform worth living" (p. 3). Parvez (2021) asserted "Attachment styles may be a strong factor influencing behavior in close relationships but they're not the only factors. Attachment theory doesn't say anything about concepts like attractiveness and mate value" (p. 7).

Operant Conditioning Theory

Operant conditioning theory is ascribed to B.F. Skinner as the originator. Ali and Soomar (2019) stated,

> Operant conditioning, which means changing behavior by providing reinforcement after desirable behavior, was presented by Skinner. Reinforcement and punishments are the most important aspects of learning. Parents use these methods to strengthen the desired behavior and weaken the undesired one. For example, if a child is being provided with his favorite toy by his or her mother for doing assignments on time, then there is the highest probability that he will repeat this behavior because of reinforcement.

On the other hand, if the child was scolded by her mother for not doing assignments on time, then she will learn that such behavior only earns condemnation and therefore she modifies her behavior accordingly. In general, a single parent focuses on earning and providing basic necessities of life to their children and tends to ignore the child's unwanted behavior that can create a problem for children in the future. So, it is very important for parents to reward desirable behavior and punish them for undesired behavior so that they can learn which behavior is good and which is not good. (p. 2)

Ali and Soomar (2019) have concluded that the "most important thing is to understand and respect the significance of parenting" (p. 3). Acknowledging this importance will certainly help in facilitating young single parents in their role as parents in Georgetown, Guyana. Acting Colleges (2022) submits "Operant conditioning does not take cognitive factors into account. Once the reward is done being given, they could go back to their bad behavior" (p. 1). Participants in the study explained that notwithstanding the rewarding efforts to their children, "Some of the children constantly cry and misbehave, and it is very frustrating for us as parents. We just do not know how to resolve it."

Family Systems Theory

A family is a whole, complex, and single system. The behaviors of each member can impact all the members of the family. Therefore, understanding the family systems and structures can greatly facilitate the process of parenting. Family systems theory is ascribed to Murray Bowen as the originator. Kerr and Bowen (as cited in Pfieffer, 2021) noted,

> It may be more beneficial to focus on the family as a whole. Family systems theory recognizes that the family plays a key role in both emotional and physical well-being across the life course since most individuals have contact with their family of origin throughout their entire lives. Families often influence day-to-day lives; families come together to both celebrate and help each other through crises. Family systems theory emphasizes the idea that families are continuous entities, with rules, beliefs, and values that shape members over time. (p. 1)

Based on the aforementioned, my study focused on providing an understanding of the value and importance of family systems for young single parents in the context of Georgetown, Guyana. This intervention sought to empower single parents with the tools to understand the dynamics of their families and focus on facilitating interactions that will enhance behaviors and improve relationships among parents and children.

Maddox (2023) opined,

All families go through challenges, whether conflict arises with parents, children, couples, or siblings. While some family conflict can be resolved without help, in many cases, family therapy can help families improve communication and move forward from conflict. In some cases, a therapist may apply the Bowen Family Systems Theory to inform family therapy techniques and support families through challenging situations. (p. 1)

Family Structure Theory

Cherry (2021) said "Structural family therapy (SFT) is a type of family therapy that looks at the structure of a family unit and improves the interactions between family members. This approach to therapy was originally developed by Salvador Minuchin" (p. 1). Cherry (2021) further stated "Addressing how much members of the family relate to one another; the goal is to improve communication and relationships to create positive changes for both individual family members and the family unit as a whole" (p. 2). This strategy is highly recommended for single-parent families. Some of the benefits of the (SFT) submitted by Cherry (2021) include "Helps individual improve their reactions to changing demands, improves communication, increases parental competence and satisfaction, and improves relationship dynamics" (p. 2). Applebury (2022) stated structural family therapy highlights "active interventions such as role-playing, requiring active participation from each member, which some may not feel comfortable with. Some strategies may cause an individual to feel singled out or sided against" (p. 2). One parent in my study insists on using the strategy of role-playing to be a role model to her daughter. Sometimes her daughter is not comfortable with what must be done, but she is shown the value of achieving the big picture.

Facilitating Competent Parenting Among Young Single Parents

Campbell (2015) asserts,

Real love is unconditional and should be evident in all love relationships see (1 Cor. 13:4-7). The foundation of a solid relationship with a child is unconditional love. Only this can assure a child's growth to full potential. Only this foundation of unconditional love can assure that such problems as feelings of resentment, being unloved, guilt, fear, and insecurity don't become significant problems. We can be confident that a child is correctly disciplined only if the parents' primary relationship with the child is one of unconditional love. Without a basis of unconditional love, it's not possible to understand a child or the child's behavior or to know how to deal with misbehavior. (p. 35)

Unconditional love is a love that is offered freely and is not based on what someone does for another person in return. This type of love is sometimes called compassionate or agape love and should be the kind of love a parent has for a child.

Campbell (2015) further, is of the view that,

Unconditional love is an ideal, we will never achieve 100 percent of the time. But again, the closer we get to it, the more satisfied and confident parents we will become, and the more satisfied, pleasant, and happy our children will be. (p. 36)

The principle of a demonstration of unconditional love provides an opportunity for young single parents in 'C' Field Sophia to improve their practices and attributes in effective child-rearing and at the same time facilitate competent parenting.

Transformational Leadership Through Empowerment for Single Parents

Van Eymeren et al. (2017) defines *transformation* as "to enable God's vision of society to be actualized in all relationships, social, economic, and spiritual so that God's will may be reflected in human society and his love be experienced by all communities, especially the poor" (p. 157).

Cherry (2020) states,

> Transformational leadership is a leadership style that can inspire positive change in those who follow. Transformational leaders are energetic, enthusiastic, and passionate. Not only are these leaders concerned and involved in the process; they are focused on helping every member of the group to succeed. (p. 1)

Reflective Leadership

Bakke Graduate University (2020) describes reflective leadership as "The leader lives in reality, reflects on its meaning, and catalyzes others with the courage, symbols, and example to make meaning in their own lives."

Van Eymeren et al. (2017) opined,

> Reflective mentors move beyond programs and activities and focus on their mentoring experience in a way that will allow them and their mentees to find meaning within the context of their relationship. Through reflection, mentors could arrive at the transformation in their lives and their mentees' lives. (p. 167)

The authors have identified the need for holistic outreach in the transformation of people, communities, and society in general. They identify reflection as a crucial component of the time that is spent with people.

Goker and Bozkus (2017) postulate,

Reflection is not only a personal process but also a collective one, which involves uncertainty along with experience and consists of specifying inquiries and essential components of a thing that came out as important, later taking a person's thoughts into dialogue with himself or herself and with other people. Individuals evaluate insights developed from that process in regard to additional perspectives, values, experiences, beliefs, and the larger context within which the questions are raised. Through reflection, newfound clarity to base changes in action or disposition is achieved. (p. 28)

The reflective leadership perspective is very applicable to the young single parents in 'C' Field Sophia Georgetown, Guyana as they reflect on their experiences, uncertainties, and values in the context of their parenting skills. The interaction from the focus-group discussions brought out new-found clarity in facilitating them in their role as parents.

Shalom Leadership

Bakke Graduate University (2020) describes shalom leadership as, "The leader pursues reconciling relationships between people, people, and God, people and their environment and people and themselves" Plantinga (as cited in Maramara, 2018) shares,

In the Bible, *shalom* means universal flourishing, wholeness, and delight-a rich state of affairs in which natural needs are satisfied and natural gifts fruitfully employed, a state of affairs that inspires joyful wonder as its Creator and Savior opens doors and welcomes the creatures in whom he delights. Shalom, in other words, is the way things ought to be. (p. 1)

Fikkert and Corbett (as cited in Van Eymeren et, al., 2017) emphasize that the goal of shalom leadership is to see people restored to being what God created them to be: people who understand that they are created in the image of God with the gifts, abilities, and capacity to make decisions and to effect change in the world around them; and people who steward their lives, communities, resources, and relationships in order to bring glory to God. (p. 171)

Shalom leadership is critical for the development of all areas of life and relationships. Therefore, the shalom leadership perspective was employed in this study to facilitate young single parents in identifying their God-given gifts. Corbett and Fikkert (2009) posit,

God created us to live in loving relationship with one another. We are not islands! We are made to know one another, to love one another, and to encourage one another to use the gifts God has given to each of us to fulfill our callings. (p. 58)

Hopefully, this transformational approach to fruitfully develop and apply those gifts will enable better parenting among young single parents.

The book of John describes Jesus meeting his disciples after the resurrection, "Yeshua, therefore, said to them again, shalom be to you. As the Father has sent me, even so, I send you" (John 20:21, HNV). Shalom experienced is multidimensional, complete well-being- physical, psychological, social, and spiritual. Shalom consists of outward peacefulness- peace between parties- and peace within.

Appreciative Inquiry Model

To introduce a transformed view of empowering young single parents in their role as parents and to provide the necessary tools to enable them to be competent in their parenting skills, one must consider the appreciative inquiry model. At its heart appreciative inquiry (AI) is about the search for the best in people, their organizations, and the strength-filled, opportunity-rich world around them. AI is a fundamental shift in the overall perspective taken throughout the entire change process to see the wholeness of the human system and to inquire into that system's strengths, possibilities, and successes.

According to Cooperrider et al. (2008) AI "is a philosophy that incorporates a process (4-D Cycle of *Discovery, Dream, Design, and Destiny*) for engaging people at any or all levels to produce effective, positive change" (p. xv). This approach is shown in Figure 1.

Figure 1

Diagram Illustrating the Appreciative Inquiry "4-D" Cycle

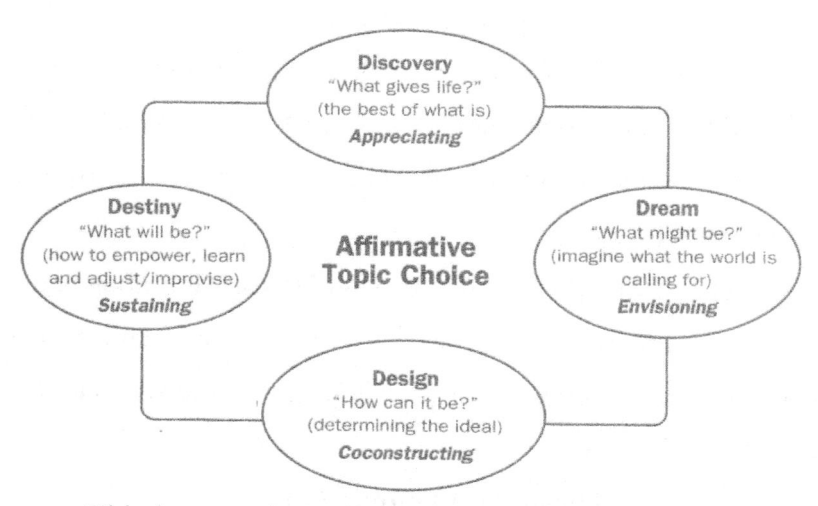

```
            Discovery
         "What gives life?"
         (the best of what is)
            Appreciating

 Destiny                      Dream
"What will be?"   Affirmative   "What might be?"
(how to empower, learn  Topic Choice  (imagine what the world is
and adjust/improvise)                  calling for)
 Sustaining                    Envisioning

              Design
          "How can it be?"
         (determining the ideal)
            Coconstructing
```

This intervention strategy is essential to the transformation process for young single parents in that it will encourage them to see solutions rather than problems and was used in the execution of the methodology of this study. Barrett and Fry (as cited in Bushe, 2021) postulate,

> A number of practitioner critiques pointed out that the 4-D model omitted an important first step in the AI process of

identifying the focus of the inquiry itself. The Clergy Leadership Institute in the U.S. suggested "Define" as the first step and some AI models refer to a 5-D model. Cooperrider's dissertation called this the "affirmative topic" and many models have retained that label. How that topic is defined has not been well articulated but is generally regarded as essential to the overall success of the effort. Engaging the right people, especially powerful sponsors, in identifying a focus that is both of high interest to those leading the organization and will be compelling to stakeholders is commonly held to be critical to overall success. (p. 3)

Bushe (2021) has concluded "After 20 years it is abundantly clear that appreciative inquiry, when skillfully done with proper sponsorship and resources, is a potent planned, transformational change process" (p. 11).

Theological Foundations

It is important to note that God's intention was for children to be raised by both mother and father. However, He also has compassion for the parent who is raising a child on his or her own. In the Bible, several single parents became parents through several circumstances. Ephesians 6:4 states, "Fathers do not exasperate your children; instead, bring them up in the training and instruction of the

Lord." The object of the apostle here is to show parents that their commands should be such that they can be easily obeyed, or such as are entirely reasonable and proper. If children are required to "obey," it is but reasonable that the commands of the parent should be such that they can be obeyed, or such that the child shall not be discouraged in his attempt to obey. Meeting children's emotional and physical needs can be overwhelming for single parents. However, there is hope and rest in the Bible to facilitate parents in their role as single parents.

The Life of Hagar

Got Questions Ministries (2022) submits,

The first single parent identified as such in the Bible is Hagar. She was an Egyptian slave who became pregnant with Abraham's child as a result of Abraham and Sarah running ahead of the Lord's instruction (Genesis 16:1-4). She was to be a surrogate, which was never God's intent. After the birth of Hagar's child, God came to Hagar in her distress and let her know that He was with her (Genesis 16:10-12). Single parents can learn what Hagar learned. When she cried out to God, He drew near. Hagar called the Lord "the God who sees me" (Genesis 16:31). Despite how lonely single parenting may be at times, those who know the Lord can take comfort in remembering that they are never alone. God promises to be a father to the fatherless and a defender of widows and orphans (Psalm 68:5). (p. 1)

Got Questions (2022) further submits "Jesus had a special tenderness for children (Matthew 19:14), and single parents can rest assured that He cares for their children as much as he does for those raised in two-parent homes" (p. 1).

The Life of Naomi

Clothed with Dignity (2020) shares the incredible story of a mother named Naomi in the Bible.

Naomi is first mentioned in the book of Ruth who was married to her husband, Elimelech. She lived in Judea with her husband and two sons, before needing to move to Moab due to a famine. While they were in Moab, Naomi's husband dies, and her sons marry two women, one of which was Ruth. After some time had passed though, both of her sons had died, and she decided to return to her homeland in Bethlehem (Ruth 1:1-5). (p. 1)

Clothed with Dignity (2020) further posits "No matter how bad things get in our lives; we don't know what the future may hold for us. We need to stay strong and focus on God, and what He has to install for us" (p. 1). The aforementioned quote was a life lesson used to encourage and facilitate single parents in their parenting.

The Life of the Widow at Zarephath

Clothed with Dignity (2020) highlights that,

The story of Prophet Elijah and the widow at Zarephath is depicted in 1 Kings 17:7-24. There was an encounter between Elijah and the widow when the widow was gathering sticks with her son. Elijah enters the town of Zarephath and asks the widow for a piece of bread. The widow invites Elijah into her home and uses every last bit of her flour and oil to make bread for him (1 Kings 17:7-13). Elijah blesses the widow and her son for doing that for him and assures her that she will not run out of supplies (1 Kings 17:14-16). (p. 1)

Clothed with Dignity (2020) proffers that the story of the widow provides encouragement for people and says "You might be in a difficult situation, but God knows the way out. Call upon Him and seek His help and guidance" (p. 1). From this example, it is clear that single parents have the propensity to make much out of little and be a blessing to others even in challenging times.

Summary

This chapter highlights the literature on Bowlby's attachment theory, Skinner's operant conditioning theory, Bowen's family system theory, and Minuchin's family structure theory. These concepts formed the theoretical framework for this book.

Central to the research was the intervention of the BGU's leadership perspective of *shalom leadership* and *reflective leadership* along with the 4-D cycle of *discovery, dream, design, and destiny* of the appreciative inquiry model that engaged participants to produce positive change. The theological foundations examined the life of single parents in the Bible such as the life of Hagar (Genesis 16:1-4), the life of Naomi (Ruth 1:1-5), and the life of the widow at Zarephath (1 Kings 17:7-24). The following chapter examines the importance of the research methodology that was used as the overarching paradigm to establish the problem and prescribe applicable solutions to facilitate single parenting.

CHAPTER 3
INVESTIGATING THE PARENTING SKILLS NEEDED TO EMPOWER YOUNG SINGLE PARENTS IN THEIR ROLE AS PARENTS

This book has addressed the problem of child-raising challenges and the critical areas of parenting skills needed to empower young single parents in their role as parents at 'C' Field Sophia in Georgetown, Guyana. I sought to establish what can be done to facilitate competent parenting among single parents, what skills do young single parents think they need to be parents, what challenges are being faced by young single parents in their role as parents and what are some strategies to facilitate the parenting skills of young single- parent families.

The Methodology

According to Sensing (2011) "The term *methodology* is the overarching paradigm the research utilizes to study a particular problem" (p. 26).

The qualitative research method was employed to conduct this study. Patton (as cited in Merriam, 2009) says,

> Qualitative research is an effort to understand situations in their uniqueness as part of a particular context and the interactions there. This understanding is an end in itself so that it is not attempting to predict what may happen in the future necessarily, but to understand the nature of that

setting- what it means for participants to be in that setting, what their lives are like, what's going on for them, what their meanings are, what the world looks like in that particular setting- and in the analysis to be able to communicate that faithfully to others who are interested in that setting...The analysis strives for depth of understanding. (p. 14)

Maanen (as cited in Merriam, 2009) defines *qualitative research* as "an umbrella term covering an array of interpretive techniques which seek to describe, decode, translate, and otherwise come to terms with the meaning, not the frequency, of certain more or less naturally occurring phenomena in the social world" (p. 13).

The qualitative inquiry and analysis of the qualitative research method was best suited for this purpose and was applied in the context of individual experiences, and subjective interpretations of the participants (Creswell & Creswell, 2018, p. 162). The qualitative approach was best suited for the Guyanese context in working with single parents in 'C' Field, Sophia. This approach was useful in understanding how single parents view the challenges of parenting in their community and how they are a part of the process of identifying workable solutions.

The Sampling Method Employed

Sensing (2011) submits "*Purposive samples* select people who have an awareness of the situation and meet the criteria and attributes that are essential to the research" (p. 83). "Patton argues that the usefulness of purposeful sampling lies in selecting 'Information-rich' cases that can provide depth to your data" (Sensing, 2011, p. 83). Merriam (2009) states, "To begin purposive sampling, you must first determine what selection criteria are essential in choosing the people or sites to be studied" (p. 77). I used the purposive sampling approach to select participants for this study. Thirty-three single parents aged 19-24 were selected from 'C' Field Sophia, Georgetown to participate in the study. Eighteen single parents participated in the one-on-one interviews, and 15 single parents participated in three focus group discussions to probe what parenting skills are needed for single parents in their parenting.

The sampling considered Sophia, a semi-urban community on the outskirts of Georgetown that has been developed for low- and middle-income housing. According to the most recently published Guyana Population and Housing Census by the Bureau of Statistics of Guyana (2012) the population of Sophia was 3,687. The age range of the sample was based on the United Nations definition of *youth* for statistical purposes as persons between the ages of 15 and 24 years. The sample then excluded persons below the age of 18, as parental consent would have been required and may have been difficult to obtain. The sample further narrowed the location within

Sophia to a single sector, that is 'C' Field Sophia, targeting both male and female single parents between 19 and 24 years of age.

The sample size was calculated based on the Sophia population of 3,687 persons adjusted for growth of 200% by 2022 translates to an estimate of 11,061 persons. Given that Sophia is subdivided into five sectors; an average of 2,220 persons per sector results in an estimated 400 single parents based on a 18% ratio of single parents to population. On this basis, 44 single parents, or 10% of the single-parent population, were targeted and actual respondents totaled 33 single parents. Tables 1, 2, and 3 depict the demographic data of the 33 respondents by age, gender, and employment status.

Table 1
Age Range of All Study Participants

	19-21 years old	22-24 years old
Number of Participants	13	20

Table 2
Gender of All Study Participants

	Male	Female
Number of Participants	5	28

Table 3

Employment Status of all Study Participants

	Employed	Unemployed
Number of Participants	48%	52%

Data-Gathering Methods

The Institutional Review Board for Research with Humans of Bakke Graduate University granted approval to conduct this research on August 15, 2022. Subsequently, letters were hand-delivered along with an attached IRB permission document to Deliverance Assembly of God Church- 'C' Field Sophia, First Assembly of God Church Judah- 'C' Field Sophia, Sophia Health Centre- 'C' Field, and 'C' Field Nursery School, seeking permission to meet with congregants who were young single parents, parents of the nursery school students, and parents who visit the Sophia Health Centre for postnatal care. These institutions were identified because of their important role in the lives of young single parents in the 'C' Field Sophia community. I was able to make several visits to these institutions to present my project and to meet with volunteers to solicit their consent to be a part of the study. Those interactions provided an opportunity for me to explain the purpose of the study, what I would ask them to do, the risks and benefits, confidentiality, and taking part voluntarily. At the end of those meetings, all 33 participants signed a Bakke Graduate University research participant consent form.

The appreciative inquiry (AI) Approach was used to design the questions for the qualitative research methods of one-on-one interviews and focus group discussions.

Cooperrider et al. (2008) submit "AI is more than crafting questions, conducting interviews, and gathering data. It is a process for engaging all relevant and interested people in positive change." Cooperrider et al. (2008) further submit "The AI 4-D Cycle is a dynamic interactive process of positive change. The 4-D Cycle of *Discovery, Dream, Design, and Destiny*" (p. 101).

One-on-one Interview

DeMarrais (as cited in Merriam, 2009) defines an *interview* as "a process in which a researcher and participant engage in a conversation focused on questions related to a research study" (p. 87). Merriam (2009) further posits "Interviewing is necessary when we cannot observe behavior, feelings, or how people interpret the world around them" (p. 88). The one-on-one interview questions are found in Appendix A. Using the data collection technique of one-on-one interviews, a total of 18 participants (16 females and 2 males) were interviewed at the Deliverance Assembly of God Church, First Assembly of God Judah, Sophia Health Centre and Demico Quick Serv Restaurant-Main Street, Georgetown.

Audio recordings were used for all the interviews with permission from the participants. From these interviews, I sought to gain insight into the participants' perceptions and understanding of what are the critical areas of parenting skills needed to empower young single parents in their role as parents; what are some of the challenges faced by young single-parent families; and what can be done to facilitate competent parenting among single parents. In the one-on-one interviews, the following qualitative open-ended questions were administered using the appreciative inquiry approach – 4 D-cycle.

Questions

Discovery

1. What is the best part of being a single parent?
2. Describe some of the challenges you face as a single parent.
3. What causes some of the challenges young single parents face?

Dream

4. Give an example of a challenge you faced as a single parent and how you addressed it.
5. What are the most essential skills young single parents need?

Design
6. If there is one experience you can share to help other young single parents in raising their children, what would it be and why?
7. What can you do to improve your parenting skills?

Destiny
8. What can be done to make parenting easier for young single parents?
9. What recommendations will you give to help young single parents become more confident as parents?

Focus Group Discussions

Sensing (2011) asserted "Group interviews are sometimes called focus groups. Through group interaction, data and insights are generated that are related to a particular theme imposed by a researcher and enriched by the group's interactive discussion" (p. 120). I conducted the focus group discussions to facilitate participants to share their personal experiences and express their feelings about their role as parents. The approach provided insight into various parenting skills, best practices, some of the challenges single parents face and a great opportunity for single parents to encourage each other in their noble responsibility of parenting.

Krueger et al. (as cited in Merriam, 2009) stated "As a method of qualitative research data collection, a focus group is an interview on a topic with a group of people who have knowledge of the topic" (p. 93). Permission was granted from Deliverance Assembly of God Church, First Assembly of God Judah, 'C' Field Sophia Nursery, and Sophia Health Centre to observe and interact with congregants, parents of the nursery school students, and young single parents receiving postnatal care from the Health Centre. After several such interactions, a sample of 15 participants (3 males and 12 females) agreed to be a part of the study and signed the Bakke Graduate University research participant consent form. The focus group discussion questions are found in Appendix B. I conducted focus group discussions for approximately 45 to 60 minutes.

The first focus group discussion was held in a private room provided by the Sophia Health Centre. The second focus group discussion was held on the premises of 'C Field Sophia Nursery School. The third focus group was held under a huge tree alongside the main access road to 'C' Field Sophia. I am grateful for the support of my wife, Mrs. Tracy Benjamin, who is a University of Guyana graduate and a member of my Personal Learning Community (PLC), who welcomed the participants of each focus group, reminded them of the strict confidentiality of views and opinions, and thanked them for participating in the discussions of investigating the critical areas of parenting skills needed to empower young single parents in their role as parents. The following qualitative open-ended questions were administered in the focus group discussions, using the appreciative inquiry approach – 4 D-cycle.

Discover
1. Share some of your peak experiences or high points in your parenting.
2. What challenges do you face in your daily child-raising experiences?
3. What are some of the reasons for the challenges faced by young single parents?

Dream
4. What is your understanding of parenting skills?
5. What are the most essential skills young single parents need to help them become more confident as parents?

Design
6. What can society do to address the challenges of young single-parent families?
7. Who do you think are the main people and institutions that can address issues of single-parent families?

Destiny
8. What can be done to improve your parenting skills?
9. What can be done to develop the practical abilities of young single parents in their parenting?

Data Analysis

Sensing (2011) defines data analysis as "the process of bringing order, structure, and meaning to the complicated mass of qualitative data that the researcher generates during the research process" (p. 194). Braun and Clarke (as cited in Kiger & Varpio, 2020) define *thematic analysis* as "a method for analyzing qualitative data that entails searching across a data set to identify, analyze, and report repeated patterns" (p. 2).

Sensing (2011) postulates "One way to organize the data is to discuss the areas of significant overlap as themes or patterns, the areas of disagreements as slippage, and the 'realities' not represented in your findings as silences" (p. 197). These were some of the strategies used to analyze the data collected in this study. The qualitative data I recorded on a Garmay Digital Voice Recorder from 18 one-on-one interviews and 3 focus group discussions, was placed in a Microsoft 365 software where the audio recordings were transcribed into a typed transcript. These sources of data gathering strengthened the process of triangulation and validity of the data and were used for further establishment of themes, patterns, and cross-tabulations in addressing the research problem and the research questions. The typed transcript of the one-on-one interviews and focus group discussions were analyzed using the Delve Tool Qualitative Data Analysis Software. Selective coding and themes resulting from the codes were further analyzed by the Delve Tool Qualitative Data Analysis to establish similar themes, cross-tabulations, frequencies, and patterns emerging from the one-on-one interviews and focus group discussions.

Evaluation

Parveen and Showkat (2017) present a module to give students a thorough understanding of the key research concepts of validity, reliability, and generalizability. Frey et al. (as cited in Parveen & Showkat, 2017) state "Validity is the 'appropriateness' of the techniques, tools, and processes; when a measure is valid, it is minimally affected by random error and systematic error. The best synonym for validity is accuracy" (p. 3). Carmines and Zeller (as cited in Parveen & Showkat, 2017) submit "Reliability is the extent to which a measurement instrument or procedure yields the same results on repeated trials" (p. 7). Polit et al. (as cited in Parveen & Showkat, 2017) state "Generalizability refers to the 'applicability' of any research findings. It means the degree to which the research study's findings can be applied to the larger samples or populations" (p. 8).

The questions that I asked were designed to garner the data for the answers needed for the study and the firsthand information collected was valid from people who are in the situation. I sought to evaluate the accuracy of the data-gathering methods and the monitoring of the effectiveness of the intervention strategies for the validity and reliability of the research by meeting with the members of my PLC team. The team provided scrutiny and feedback on my work in the study by not allowing my own biases or perceptions to affect the process. The team further scrutinized and finalized the questions used in the data-gathering methods before I engaged the participants. A member of the PLC team was appointed as a scribe for all the focus group discussions (FGD) and I also engaged a qualified social worker who led most of the discussions in the second session of the empowerment seminar and gave valuable feedback on the overall research process. The (PLC) team also assisted in interpreting and presenting the findings of the data tables, graphs, and charts. The one-on-one interviews highlighted each participant's in-depth and personalized experiences, while the focus discussions highlighted the participant's beliefs, views, and perceptions of the critical areas of parenting skills needed to empower them in their role as young single parents in 'C' Field Sophia, Georgetown, Guyana. In examining the reliability of the data received, I also considered the consistency of several responses such as employment status. Even though this study focused on young single parents in the community of 'C' Field Sophia, I believe that the research approach can be used in other communities as it relates to investigating the challenges young single parents face and exploring ways to mitigate those challenges.

Ethical Considerations

According to Merriam (2009), "In any qualitative study, ethical issues relating to the protection of the participants are of concern" (p. 161). Merriam further submits "The term *participants* are commonly used by qualitative researchers to describe the individuals being studied. It is a carefully chosen identifier, with connotations of inclusion and willing cooperation" (p. 162).

The single-parent population is vulnerable, and I addressed sensitive family issues. As mentioned earlier, each participant in the study signed the Bakke Graduate University research participant consent form and was assured that their names would not be used. Each participant was referred to by a number between 1 to 33. Participants were briefed on strict adherence to their confidentiality. Therefore, all the research records, including audio recordings, are safely stored in a locked cabinet. Participants were also informed that if for any reason they were unable to complete an interview, they were free to discontinue the interview.

The Transformational Strategy Employed

It was very important to get a consensus and an agreement from the participants on the possible time and date that was suitable for the execution of the empowerment seminar. Therefore, during the interviews and focus group discussions participants were given time to consider a date and time for the seminar. On October 22, 2022, I was able to organize and execute an in-person empowerment seminar with a focus on participants' personal growth and development at First Assembly of God Judah Church. Based on the findings of the study, participants expressed the need to pursue an area of personal growth and development in their lives. Participants also expressed that due to the reality of parenting, the focus on their personal growth and development has been placed on hold. However, the participants are determined to pursue their personal growth and development so that they can empower themselves and their children.

The Format of the Seminar

The objectives of the seminar were to

1. inspire young single parents to engage in the process of personal growth and development that will transform their lives and

2. provide a safe space for parents to share their experiences and co-create dreams for their families.

The seminar was divided into two sessions. The first session was in the form of a PowerPoint presentation, and the second session was in the form of an activity for the participants.

The First Session

In a PowerPoint presentation entitled Definition and Key Terms Used in the Seminar, I addressed the following topics.

1. Empowerment- the process of becoming stronger and more confident, especially in controlling one's life and claiming one's rights
2. SMART goals- Specific, Measurable, Attainable, Realistic & Timely
3. Personal Growth and Development- the ongoing process of self-improvement.

It involves the enhancement of different aspects of your life, such as how you view yourself and your effectiveness in living. It includes developing positive life skills and realistic self-esteem.

4. Why is Personal Growth and Development Important?
   - Learning to better control your emotions and negative thoughts
   - Overcoming procrastination or laziness
   - Being open to learning new skills
   - Having a "growth mindset"
   - Finding peace and contentment with things you cannot change
5. The Appreciative Inquiry Model
   - Discover

- Dream
- Design
- Destiny

6. Questions and Answers

The Second Session

Of the 33 participants of the study, 12 participants (2 males and 10 females) attended and participated in an activity to focus on their personal growth and development. For approximately two hours, each participant was given a questionnaire to document one area of personal growth and development in their lives and the strategy to accomplish this goal. The questions were designed using the appreciative inquiry approach of the 4 D- cycle. The areas highlighted were 1) an area of personal growth and development, 2) an institution to attend to achieve this goal, 3) a short-term plan to achieve this goal, and 4) how the participants saw themselves in 1 to 3 years from now.

Interventions and Observations

I received critical support in the execution of the much-anticipated activity from the participants. My wife Tracy Benjamin, Mr. Wesley Adams a social worker, and Mrs. Faye Adams a Systems Analyst provided critical support in the PowerPoint presentation, the distribution of questionnaires, and assistance in completing the questionnaires. The seminar proved that the participants were allowed to realize their potential. They were engaged in areas of study that will help in self-development and further provide an opportunity for them to learn new skills and earn additional income. A remarkable observation was that several mothers brought their children to the seminar.

The reason was they were unable to get anyone to take care of the children while they were away. The display of determination and resilience was admirable in making a positive change in their lives. The guidance given coupled with the methodology helped the participants not only identify their strengths and weaknesses but also enlighten them in such a manner that they were able to identify the areas of skill training that are best suited for them. For example, the two young fathers who attended the seminar demonstrated their interest in being trained in heavy-duty machinery, as drivers and operators. The willingness of these young single parents coming from a community that is considered a depressed community is an encouragement to ensure that this project was a success. Through this initiative, the hope is that other young single parents will be reached spanning other communities throughout Guyana as a means of providing the best opportunity for training and self-development. The interactions during the activity engendered an opportunity for the participants to share their experiences and encouraged each other not to give up on their role of parenting. Participants shared their contact numbers to stay in contact with each other and started a WhatsApp group to bring critical support that is needed.

The seminar ended with participants being provided with lunch and the submission of a duplicate of the completed questionnaire to facilitate a follow-up process. Participants were inspired and motivated to follow through with their personal growth and development plans. Participants further expressed the experience of a mindset change and received the tools needed to realize their goals. Participants left the seminar with a mindset change and the necessary tools needed to start the process of their personal growth and development.

Summary

This chapter describes the overall research design, the purposive sampling methods, data gathering and analysis, and the ethical considerations that authenticate this study. The data were coded and analyzed using the Delve Tool Qualitative Data Analysis Software to determine frequencies, patterns, behaviors, and relationships. This approach helped to identify what can be done to facilitate competent parenting among single parents, identified and determined the impact of the challenges faced, how to overcome these challenges, and the relevant strategies needed to facilitate parenting skills to empower young single parents. The transformational strategy was highlighted along with an evaluation of the effectiveness of the study. The following chapter highlights the findings and results presented.

CHAPTER 4
DISCOVERING THE REALITIES OF SINGLE PARENTING

This chapter provides a detailed report on the findings and results of the analysis of this study. The qualitative research method was applied and utilized the data gathering procedures of one-on-one interviews and focus group discussions. The analysis further reports on the transcribed text from 18 one-on-one interviews and 3 focus group discussions of young single parents of 'C' Field Sophia Georgetown, Guyana, between the ages of 19 and 24. The Delve Qualitative analysis software was used to identify the emergent themes in the interviews and the focus group discussions. The transcribed text was analyzed from the audio recordings of the interviews.

Demographics of the Participants

A total of 18 participants responded to questions in the one-on-one interviews as depicted in Table 4.

Table 4

Demographics of Participants by Gender

Gender	No.	%
Male	2	11%
Female	16	89%
Total	**18**	**100%**

As depicted in Figure 2, there were two male (11%) and sixteen female (89%) participants, showing an overwhelming majority of females conducted the interviews.

Figure 2

Gender of Participants

Gender of Participants

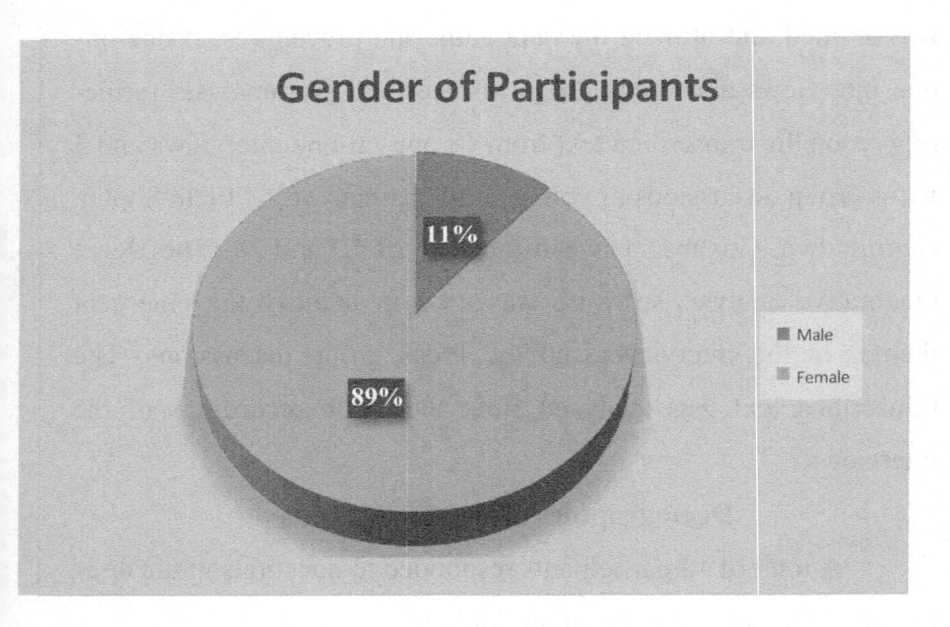

- 11% Male
- 89% Female

As presented in Table 5, 9 participants were between the ages of 19 and 21 years old, while 9 participants were between the ages of 22 and 24 years old, providing a good mix of perspectives by age.

Table 5

Age Range of Participants

	19-21 years old	22-24 years old
Number of Participants	9	9

Table 6 reflects the employment status with 10 participants who are currently employed (56%), and 8 participants who are currently unemployed (44%). Each participant signed a consent form and was assigned a number from 1 to 18.

Table 6

Employment Status of Participants

	Employed	Unemployed
Number of Participants	56%	44%

Themes Emerging from Responses to the Interviews

This subsection highlighted the responses from the one-on-one interviews. Themes are important in research since they help to identify commonalities in the data collection process and capture the main idea of the purpose of the research. As such, the following figures and tables capture responses that were not mutually exclusive but rather captured the number of similar responses that informed the emerging themes.

Theme 1: The close bond shared between parents and children

This theme is in response to question 1: What is the best part of being a single parent? This question is categorized under the discover stage of the 4 D-cycle in the appreciative inquiry approach of the structuring of the questions for the qualitative research method of one-on-one interviews. Eleven of the 18 participants (61%) interviewed referred to the close bond shared between parents and children and further expressed the feeling of joy and happiness they experience while being in the presence of their children and the observance of laughter upon the faces of their children. The following are comments from participants relating to question 1.

Participant # 5: "The consistent involvement in the growth and development of your children and the importance of being there for them."

Participant # 9: "The best part is getting to know your child. Knowing how to make her happy and what to do when she is sad. The bond that you have as a mother and a child is very satisfying."

Participant # 18: "The love and care that is shared between the parents and the children are special. It forms a close bond."

Theme 2: Meeting the daily needs of my children

This theme came out of responses to question 2, "Describe some of the challenges you face as a single parent." Single parents face many challenges in the daily responsibility of taking care of their children. The challenges faced can sap their energy physically and emotionally. How single parents address these challenges would require a positive mindset to help them redirect the energy needed in raising their children. Table 7 reveals the findings that 10 of the 18 participants (56%) interviewed stated that meeting the daily needs of their children was a major challenge. Some participants described the challenges as, not having a permanent job to adequately provide for the daily needs of the children, preparing the children on a timely basis for school, and not being able to provide meals for the children.

Table 7

Participant Responses to Question 2: Describe some of the challenges you face as a single parent

Responses	Number of responses	Percentage
Meeting daily needs	10	56%
Lack of parenting skills needed to empower single parents	6	33%
Lack of family support	7	39%

The following views were expressed by some of the participants regarding the challenges they face in meeting the daily needs of their children.

Participant # 1: "As a mother, well some days things would be really difficult waking up with nothing to eat. Some days there are some things that your kids would be in need of, and you're not able to find them or provide them." **Participant# 7:** "My challenge is mostly financial. Not having enough finances to provide for my daughter. At present, it is not easy at all to provide for her and care for her when she is sick."

Participant# 17: "The lack of finances to raise three children."

Theme 3: Lack of parenting skills

This theme is in response to question 2. Describe some of the challenges you face as a single parent. The study findings revealed that 6 of the 18 participants (33%) have challenges with the necessary parenting skills needed to empower them in their role as young single parents. The following are perspectives of participants regarding their lack of parenting skills as a major challenge they face as single parents.

Participant # 11: "I don't know how to deal with my child crying over insignificant things."

Participant # 14: "It is overwhelming having to deal with raising this child by myself."

Participant # 15: "Being overwhelmed sometimes with my daily chores and having to deal with raising this child by myself."

Theme 4: Lack of family support

This theme came out of the responses to question 2. Describe some of the challenges you face as a single parent. The findings in this study revealed that 7 of the 18 participants (39%) view the lack of family support as a major challenge they face as single parents. Here are some of the responses.

Participant # 4: "One such challenge is the fear of wondering and thinking if I'm being judged in the way I raise my child by my family and society. I don't know if they're expecting me to be perfect because they look into every little thing I do."

Participant # 8: "I experience bad family relations with the father of my children and his family. They are very abusive to me. It sometimes ends up in a physical fight between us."

Participant # 9: "Getting someone to take care of my daughter while I go to work and further my studies. I could not afford to pay for daycare. You must think about their well-being and if the child is comfortable."

Theme 5: No co-parenting

Family impacts one another to some extent, and what happens to one will positively or negatively impact others, affecting their thoughts, feelings, and behaviors. (Regain Editorial Team, 2023). Of the 18 participants interviewed, 10 of them (56%-all mothers) expressed the reality of no co-parenting as the main reason for question 3. What causes some of the challenges faced by young single parents? During several interviews, there were expressions of anger and disgust, and becoming emotional with the shedding of tears by the mothers who are still trying to deal with the magnitude of the situation of not having the father of their children playing a role in the upbringing of their children. The following responses were made to the following question. What causes some of the challenges young single parents face?

Participant # 1: "Not having any help from the other parent."

Participant # 2: "The father's denial of the child and the father's parents' denial of the child."

Participant # 6: "The fathers not playing a role in the lives of the children."

Participant # 7: "The lack of co-parenting. Abusive relationship. The responsibility to raise this child is on me."

Participant # 8: "The father of my child and his parents are not appreciative of the efforts I am making to raise my child."

Participant # 9: "The lack of co-parenting."

Participant # 11: "Absentee father not playing any role in the upbringing of the child."

Theme 6: Financial burden

This theme emerged from the response to question 4. Give an example of a challenge you faced as a single parent and how you addressed it. The findings of this study expressed in Table 8 revealed that 8 of 18 participants (44%) interviewed equally identified finances and personal development as challenges in their daily parenting experiences. Swindoll (1990) opined, "Finances. The cost of bearing, clothing, feeding, entertaining, and educating children is the greatest in our history" (p. 17).

Table 8

Participant Responses to Question 4: Give an example of a challenge you faced as a single parent and how you addressed it.

Responses	Number of responses	%
Financial burden	8	44%
Balancing personal development and parenting	8	44%

Participants challenged themselves to do something to change the situation, reached out to family members for help to meet an urgent need for the child, and in some instances left themselves undone to ensure that the children were taken care of. The following comments are participants' expressions of addressing the financial burden experienced.

Participant # 1: "Well financial instability, and I was able to overcome that by challenging myself to do things. I was unemployed, and I started making pastries to sell, farming the yard, and selling the produce I was able to overcome financial instability by making myself useful."

Participant # 12: "I didn't have anything to give my son for his meal to take to school. However, I contacted my elder brother and he assisted in providing some finances for my son to get a meal to take to school."

Theme 7: Balancing personal development and parenting

This theme emerged from the response to question 4. Give an example of a challenge you faced as a single parent and how you addressed it. Evidence suggests that young single parents display an indomitable spirit in making decisions every day to bring a balance between their personal development and their responsibilities of parenting.

They find ways to center themselves, mentally, socially, and emotionally in keeping themselves strong during stressful moments and being a good example to their children. Of the 18 participants interviewed 8 participants (44%) shared their experiences in addressing the challenge of balancing personal development and parenting. The following comments are participants' expressions of addressing balancing personal development and parenting.

Participant #3: "I furthered my studies and am now in a better position and earning power to help to provide and meet the daily needs of my child. I am now better equipped to teach my child values and life skills that will help to overcome her own challenges in life."

Participant # 9: "Balancing my studies and having to take care of my daughter. I failed my exams. It was difficult. I did not have the support in taking care of my daughter. It was a stressful time for me. I addressed it by giving myself more time to prepare for the second attempt at the exams. I had to wean her from me and teach her that it is ok to be without me sometimes. Friends offered help in taking care of her."

Theme 8: Giving love and affection

This theme emerged from the response to question 5. What are the most essential skills young single parents need? In Table 9 at least five skills were deemed as essential to single parents with 8 of 18 participants interviewed or 44% highlighting love and affection as one of the most essential skills needed in their role as parents.

Table 9

Participant Responses to Question 5: What are the most essential skills young single parents need?

Responses	Number of responses	%
Love & Affection	8	44%
Safe & Secure Environment	2	11%
Exercising patience	2	11%
Disciplining children	2	11%
Spending quality time with children	4	22%

The following comments represent responses from participants regarding the most essential skills needed.

Participant # 1: "Giving love and affection to your children, coping skills to address the needs of your children, and managing the daily stress of providing for them, learning how to listen to your children. It is important to love your children. If they are not loved, they will be looking for love elsewhere and that can expose them to danger. For example, sometimes if they can't get love and affection in the house they would go over by a neighbor."

Participant # 8: "Parents need to pay attention to the changes that are taking place in the lives of their children. Give love and affection, spend quality time with the children, teach your children how to read and write, teach them morals, and teach them how to cope with life in general. This will enable them to be a better person."

Participant # 18: "Giving love and care will help the children to feel comfortable and secure."

Theme 9: Providing a safe and secure environment

This theme emerged from the response to question 5. What are the most essential skills young single parents need? Providing a place where children are physically, emotionally, and socially secure is critical in the process of them reaching their full potential. It helps to establish meaningful relationships and a feeling of connection with their parents. The study findings revealed that participants view this responsibility as an essential skill that is needed by parents. More importantly, participants opined that the practice of this skill is a vital part of children's growth and development in the future.

Participants also are of the view that the little things they do and say to their children give them a comfort level to be open with them as parents. The study findings showed that of the 18 participants interviewed, 2 participants (11%) stated that providing a safe and secure environment is an essential skill young single parents need. The following comments represent responses from participants regarding the most essential skill needed.

Participant #11: "Learning how to make your children feel satisfied and comfortable in the home."

Participant #18: "Giving love and care will help the children to feel comfortable and secure."

Theme 10: Exercising patience

This theme emerged from the response to question 5. What are the most essential skills young single parents need? Parents need to exercise patience in the day-to-day upbringing of their children. Parents who discover this essential skill have a better understanding of the struggle and difficulty of everyday life and use a more patient approach than a complaining approach in their role as parents. A necessary part of parenting is the investment of time and patience in shaping the future of their children.

The evidence from the study suggests that the application of patience is paramount to the reduction of stress in their parenting experiences. It is also noteworthy that parents view exercising patience as a test of managing their own stress and improving their self-esteem. Of the 18 participants interviewed, 2 participants (11%) perceived exercising patience as an essential skill young single parents need. The following comments represent responses from participants regarding the most essential skills needed.

Participant # 7: "Single parents need patience; they need hope to see beyond the current situation and that things will be better in raising their children because they just must be there for them."

Participant # 9: "Patience- when the children are young, they are now learning, they are all different so as a young single parent, you need to give time to your child to develop."

Theme 11: How to discipline your child

This theme emerged from the response to question 5. What are the most essential skills young single parents need? Of the 18 participants interviewed, 2 participants (11%) suggested how disciplining their children is an essential skill needed by young single parents. In this study, the responses suggest that young single parents need guidance from older parents in the community in learning how to discipline their children. The following comment represents the response from a participant regarding the most essential skills needed.

Participant # 3: "Putting a system in place for counseling sessions for parents to learn more about parenting. Guidance and teaching from older parents in the community. Learning how to discipline your child. Bringing a balance between corporal punishment and using other methods to discipline the child."

Theme 12: Spending quality time with your children

This theme emerged from the response to question 5. What are the most essential skills young single parents need? It may be more beneficial to focus on the family.

Family systems theory recognizes that the family plays a key role in both emotional and physical well-being across the life course since most individuals have contact with their family of origin throughout their entire lives (Pfieffer, 2021). Parents spending quality time with their children is a demonstration of their love and care for them and is also important to the children since it plays a key role in their well-being. Of the 18 participants interviewed, 4 participants (22%) are of the view that spending quality time with their children is an essential skill needed by young single parents. The following are the responses of participants in the study.

Participant # 9: "Being a role model to your children is very important. You need to keep a certain standard of living by doing some simple things such as being kind for them to see and practice."

Participant # 12: "How to teach your children the necessary skills to help them grow and develop."

Participant # 13: "Manage, and monitor what your children are reading, and looking at on the television and cell phones."

Theme 13: Manage your spending

This theme emerged from the response to question 6. If there is one experience you can share to help other young single parents in raising their children, what would it be and why? The findings of this study revealed that the reality of handling unexpected bills and managing everyday expenses is exceedingly difficult. Sometimes it adds to the stress of taking control and managing the limited available resources. Of the 18 participants interviewed, 5 participants (28%) expressed the view that managing spending is a key area to pay attention to in the child-raising experience of young single parents.

The following are the responses of participants in the study.

Participant # 1: "One of the experiences that I had as a single parent was not being able to give my kids everything they needed. I overcame that by working by myself. It helped me to be closer to my kids because I did not have to go out and work and leave them with anybody or leave them unattended. I had them close to me. Other single parents, rather than just staying home and just staying home and just doing nothing can develop some skills and earn an income to help raise their children. Finally, learn how to manage your finances. You can sell twenty trays of ice at $20.00 per tray in a day. That means an income of $400.00 and you can save $200.00 of the amount after taking care of expenses. This gives a daily financial support or can be kept to see how you gained by the end of the month." **Participant # 9:** "To save money, I used public transportation to take my child to the daycare and walked to and from work to pick her up. That experience taught me resilience. I had to make it work for my daughter. My aim was to show my daughter if mommy can do this then she can do anything. It also taught me that it is ok for parents to take risks."

Theme 14: Prioritizing my well-being

This theme emerged from the response to question 6. If there is one experience you can share to help other young single parents in raising their children, what would it be and why? Young single parents need to pay attention to their own needs and well-being. The pressure of child-rearing can mount from day to day and can have a negative impact on the physical and mental health of parents. Parents are therefore encouraged to have a positive outlook on themselves and focus on finding meaning and joy in their daily child-raising experiences. Table 10 highlights the two themes that emerged from question 6 with 5 of 18 (28%) participants interviewed having expressed the necessity for self-care and that it should be a part of their daily routine. A similar number of responses also highlighted managing your spending, making finance a common theme from preceding question responses.

Table 10

Participant Responses to Question 6: If there is one experience you can share to help other young single parents in raising their children, what would it be and why?

Responses	Number of responses	%
Manage your spending	5	28%
Prioritizing my well-being	5	28%

The following is the response of a participant in the study.

Participant # 7: "They need to be fighters. Do not give up on yourself. Take care of yourself. Not to disappoint the child, not to give up on the child. They need to wake up every morning with that determination to fight for the child's growth and development. This is so because at the end of the day, it is your child and you have the responsibility to raise a healthy child. It is also important to be a good role model to the child. This is because they look up to you as the parent for an example in life."

Theme 15: Improving communication skills

This theme emerged from the response to question 7. What can you do to improve your parenting skills? Creating an environment for good communication between parents and children is one of the key factors that influence a positive relationship and more interactions between the parents and the children. It also helps to develop children's understanding of their emotional, social, and cultural well-being. Of the 18 participants interviewed, 8 participants (44%) expressed the need to improve their communication skills, which will be a great asset to their role as parents. The following are some of the responses of participants in the study.

Participant # 4: "Because I'm still a young mother, there are several areas that I'm still learning. I need to learn to listen and take advice. I need to learn how to take care of another life. I'm learning how to care for him and his stuff but, I'm still on my way to learning."

Participant # 7: "I must improve my mental health. I suffer from anxiety, and it causes me to become angry and frustrated and want to react negatively. This happens when things aren't going according to plan."

Participant # 12: "Form a family group (siblings and cousins) to constantly communicate with each other on the experiences of raising our children and seek to learn and implement the best practices where applicable."

Participant # 13: "Practicing good manners to teach my daughter by observation."

Theme 16: Multitasking

This theme emerged from the response to question 7. What can you do to improve your parenting skills? The courageous skill of being able to do more than one thing at a time and doing it well is a real test of strength and ability for young single parents. This type of practice has helped several parents become more capable of handling the day-to-day responsibility of parenting so that their day can run smoothly and safely for themselves and their children. Reports in the study revealed that participants are learning the skill of multitasking, and there is a need to place more emphasis on improving it as a part of their parenting skills. Table 11 highlights two themes emerging from responses to question 7. Of the 18 participants interviewed, 6 participants (33%) expressed the view that multitasking is what they can do to improve their parenting skills while a higher number of 8 participants signaled communication as an area for improvement.

Table 11

Participant Responses to Question 7. What can you do to improve your parenting skills?

Responses	Number of responses	%
Improving communication	8	44%

skills		
Multitasking	6	33%

The following are some of the responses of participants in the study.

Participant # 3: "Reading more about life skills, parenting, etc. Socializing more with other young single parents to learn more about parenting and learning more about what is needed for a healthy childhood for my child."

Participant # 9: "Learn from your everyday experiences in raising the child and repeat those best practices."

Participant # 18: "Give more love and care to my children and remain focused on meeting their daily needs."

Theme 17: Have a "can do" attitude

This theme emerged from the response to question 8. What can be done to make parenting easier for young single parents? Having a "can do" attitude is a very important skill needed by young single parents in their role as parents. This approach of a positive attitude helps single parents highlight and focus on the best practices rather than focusing on the negatives. More importantly, it increases their competence in parenting. The findings in the study have shown that young single parents in 'C' Field Sophia have adopted this approach and are taking note of the efforts and small achievements they are making and are of the view that having a "can do" attitude is one of the most critical areas of parenting that needs to be encouraged. Of the 18 participants interviewed, 7 (39%) participants have expressed the view that a "can do" attitude is paramount in making parenting easier for young single parents. The following are some of the responses of participants in the study.

> **Participant # 2:** "Form community groups where the older parents and citizens can mentor young single, share their experiences, and give practical examples of effective parenting which can be used as tools for better parenting by young single parents."
>
> **Participant # 3:** "Learn from the success stories in the daily experiences in raising your child and repeat them as much as possible."
>
> **Participant # 9:** "Pre-planning and buying in bulk is important in purchasing the necessities to raise your child."

Theme 18: Know your limitations

This theme emerged from the response to question 8. What can be done to make parenting easier for young single parents? The findings revealed that several participants acknowledged that it is very difficult to fulfill the role of parenting all alone. Training in parenting, counseling, and family support are some of the key areas identified where help is needed. Some participants feel helpless in their efforts to give their children a healthy life and future. Of the 18 participants interviewed, 8 participants (44%) expressed the view that knowing your limitations is important in the process of seeking help to make parenting easier for young single parents in the 'C' Field Sophia area. Table 12 captures this view by single parents with a similar view even if a lesser number of 39% signaling a 'can do attitude' as needed to make single parenting easier.

Table 12

Participant Responses to Question 8. What can be done to make parenting easier for young single parents?

Responses	Number of responses	%
Have a "can do" attitude	7	39%
Know your limitations	8	44%

The following are some of the responses of participants in the study.

Participant #1: "Provide counseling for young single parents. They really need help. Sometimes there is no one to talk to on issues that they are going through. Like how to raise children, how to train them, teach them manures, etc."

Participant # 4: "More training in parenting can be done. Classes etc. to help young single parents to become better parents."

Participant # 16: "They need encouragement and motivation in fulfilling their responsibilities."

Theme 19: Ask for help

This theme emerged from the response to question 9. What recommendations will you give to help young single parents become more confident as parents? Single parents are vulnerable as all are in various ways. They need to know that it's ok to ask for help, and it is not a sign of weakness. Getting support is critical and helpful for the parent and the child, and it expresses the feeling that people do care about them. Of the 18 participants interviewed, 7 participants (39%) expressed the need for support physically, emotionally, and socially. The following are some of the responses of participants in the study.

>**Participant # 1:** "Be patient with your children as they learn new things every day. Have a "can do" attitude to your daily chores. Be willing to ask for help, not be too hard on yourself, be prepared to build a lifetime of strong relationships with your children, and don't be afraid of failure. Just keep trying and you will succeed and become more confident with time."
>
>**Participant # 6:** "Society can give good advice on how to manage the demands at work and at home. Teach us coping skills with all the demands of parenting."
>
>**Participant # 18:** "Surround yourself with people who can help you to elevate and educate yourself."

Theme 20: Celebrate the achievements in your parenting

This theme emerged from the response to question 9. What recommendations will you give to help young single parents become more confident as parents? Reflective mentors move beyond programs and activities and focus on their mentoring experience in a way that will allow them and their mentees to find meaning within the context of their relationship (Van Eymeren et al. 2017). As mentors to their children, the young single parents of 'C' Field Sophia can reflect on the experience of achieving a goal or completing a simple task in parenting. It is always good to reflect on one's accomplishments as a parent. Sometimes it's easy to get caught up in the failures and shortcomings experienced in the daily child-raising process. However, when time is given to reflect on and celebrate the small wins, it reinforces self-esteem and motivates parents to be more competent in their parenting. The findings in the study indicate that several participants believe that taking the time to celebrate their achievements in their role as parents can boost the competence that is needed in their everyday approach to parenting. Table 13 highlights the two emerging themes in responses to question 9.

Table 13

Participant Responses to Question 9. What recommendations will you give to help young single parents become more confident as parents?

Responses	Number of responses	%
Ask for help	7	39%
Celebrate the achievements in your parenting	6	33%

Of the 18 participants interviewed, 6 participants (33%) expressed the view that celebrating the achievements in parenting is a recommendation to help young single parents become more confident as parents. A higher percentage response of 39% indicated asking for help as a recommendation to build confidence as a parent. The following is a response from a participant in the study.

Participant # 8: "Engage your children from a young age in what they want to become in life and help them to choose a career path."

Demographics of Participants in the Focus Group Discussions

A total of 15 participants responded to questions in the focus group discussions.

Focus group #1 (FG#1)

This group comprised four females. Table 14 depicts 2 participants between the ages of 19 and 21 years old (50%) and 2 participants between the ages of 22 and 24 years old (50%). The participants' employment status was split evenly, with 50% employed versus 50% unemployed. Each participant signed a consent form and was assigned a number from 19 to 22.

Table 14

The Age Range of Participants in Focus Group 1

Age Range	Number of participants	%
19 - 21 years old	2	50%
22 - 24 years old	2	50%

Focus group #2 (FG#2)

This group comprised four females. Table 15 depicts 1 participant between the ages of 19 and 21 years old (25%) and 3 participants between the ages of 22 and 24 years (75%).

Table 15

The Age Range of Participants in Focus Group 2

Age Range	Number of participants	%
19 - 21 years old	1	25%
22 - 24 years old	3	75%

Table 16 illustrates that a higher percentage of the participants are currently employed (75%), while 1 participant is currently unemployed (25%). Each participant signed a consent form and was assigned a number from 23 to 26.

Table 16

Employment Status of Participants in Focus Group 2

	Employed	Unemployed
Number of Participants	75%	25%

Focus Group #3 (FG#3)

The composition of the group included three males (43%) and four females (57%) in this group. Table 17 depicts the age range with 1 participant under the age of 19 and 21 (14%), and 6 participants between the ages of 22 and 24 years old (86%).

Table 17

Age Range of Participants in Focus Group 3

Age Range	Number of participants	%
19 - 21 years old	1	14%
22 - 24 years old	6	86%

Table 18 shows the employment status of this focus group with six participants currently employed (86%), and one participant currently unemployed (14%). Each participant signed a consent form and was assigned a number from 27 to 33.

Table 18

Employment Status of Participants in Focus Group 3

	Employed	Unemployed
Number of Participants	86%	14%

83

Themes Emerging from Responses to the Focus Group Discussions

This sub-section highlighted the responses from the focus group discussions. Themes are important in research since they help to identify commonalities in the data collection process and capture the main idea of the purpose of the research.

Theme 1: Becoming a parent

This theme emerged from the response to question 1. Share some of your peak experiences or high points in your parenting. There is so much to say about becoming a parent. It can be one of the most emotional, fulfilling, and exciting experience in your life. It is a tremendous responsibility. Some parents have summed up this responsibility with the word *influence,* which is being able to influence a child's life and future positively. Table 19 shows that of the 15 participants in the FG discussions, 5 participants (33%) described the experience of becoming a parent as a high point in their parenting, while 4 participants (27%) described the bond shared between parents and children as their peak experience.

Table 19

Peak Experiences in Your Parenting

Peak Experiences in your parenting	Number of responses	%
Becoming a parent	5	33%

| The strong bond shared between parents and children | 4 | 27% |
| Total Participants | 15 | 100% |

Participant # 20 (FG#1): "I rallied out and finally gave birth to a bouncing baby girl. So that was a peak moment for me. I am proud of myself that I managed that pain and delivered my daughter with no complications."

Participant # 26 (FG#2): "Taking care of my children is a high point for me. I take my responsibility seriously. I love to see them happy. The first time they said mom was a high point for me."

Participant # 31 (FG#3): "Becoming a father was a high point in my parenting."

Theme 2: The strong bond shared between parents and children

This theme emerged from the response to question 1. Share some of your peak experiences or high points in your parenting. Attachment is a basic human need for a secure relationship between children and caregivers (Ali & Soomer, 2019). The study identified the importance of the parent-child relationship. Parenting can be one of the most fulfilling jobs because it creates an opportunity to nurture and form a unique bond that is needed for every child. Of the 15 participants in the FG discussions, 4 participants (27%)

highlighted the value of a strong bond shared between parents and children as a peak experience in their parenting. The following are responses from participants in the study.

Participant #23 (FG#2): "Some of my peak experiences as a single parent would be the greetings I receive from my children upon arrival from work. The hugs and kisses, the love shown by them are very special to me. It makes you forget that you are doing it all alone. And motivates you to do more. If it were another way around where the father was there, I would have accepted it. But I would not trade them for the world."

Participant # 32 (FG#3): "To wake up in the morning and see my children around me and bond with them is nice."

Participant # 30 (FG#3): "Being able to work and take care of my children brings me joy."

Theme 3: Providing for the daily needs of the children

This theme emerged from the response to question 2. What are some of the challenges you face in your daily child-raising experiences? Single parents may experience the challenges of attempting to fulfill the role of two parents as a sole person and income earner (Better Health Channel, 2022). This reality was highlighted in the study as several participants expressed the view that it is very difficult to provide for the daily needs of the children.

Table 20 highlights 6 of 15 (40%) FG participants shared their experiences in providing for the children, while 27% shared on lack of family support as a challenge.

Table 20

Challenges You Face in Your Daily Child-raising Experiences

Challenges you face in your daily child-raising experiences	Number of responses	%
Providing for the daily needs of the children	6	40%
Lack of family support	4	27%
Total Participants	15	100%

Participant# 21 (FG#1): "Providing meals for my child daily. Some days it is difficult to find milk, food, pampers, etc. I have to manage the limited resources I have."

Participant # 23 (FG#2): "Providing 3 meals a day for my children is a challenge. Some days I can't, and the children are crying."

Participant # 31 (FG#3): "Things are rough financially. The balance of paying bills and providing for my children."

Theme 4: Lack of family support

This theme emerged from the response to question 2. What are some of the challenges you face in your daily child-raising experiences? Families often influence day-to-day lives (Pfieffer,

2021). Family support is necessary for maintaining good health, and a lack thereof often causes some parents to feel isolated and has a negative impact on their mental health. The study revealed that the lack of family support is one of the daily child-raising challenges young single parents face in 'C' Field Sophia. Of the 15 participants in the FG discussions, 4 participants (27%) expressed the view that the lack of family support was a major challenge. The following are responses from participants in the study.

Participant # 22 (FG#1): "Support in raising my child."

Participant # 20 (FG#1): "I need alone time to think and be free from the daily routine of parenting. However, there is nobody that I can depend on to monitor my child for me to experience that alone time."

Participant # 33 (FG#3): "I must do it alone. No relationship with the father."

Theme 5: No co-parenting

This theme emerged from the response to question 3. What are some of the reasons for the challenges faced by young single parents? Parents who are in a good co-parenting relationship help to raise their children in a secure and loving environment.

This practice also fosters many benefits for the well-being of the children. The study revealed some of the consequences of no co-parenting as participants expressed their views on some of the reasons for the challenges faced by young single parents. Forty percent (6 of 15) participants in the FG discussions shared their experiences of a lack of or no co-parenting as a challenge.

> The following are responses from participants in the study.
> **Participant # 20 (FG#1):** "Support in caring for the child from the father. Sometimes they support them financially, but they need to be actively involved in the lives of their children to bring guidance to them."
> **Participant # 22 (FG#1):** "No support from the father."
> **Participant# 26 (FG#2):** "Because of the nonparticipation of the fathers of the children I became angry with them and myself. This behavior is affecting me in not showing positive emotions toward my children. I find myself snapping at my children."

Theme 6: The ability to administer care for your children

This theme emerged from the response to question 4. What is your understanding of parenting skills? The process of raising a child from birth to adulthood is a parental responsibility that must be taken seriously and must be understood by parents. The study captured the perception of participants' understanding of parenting skills. Of the 15 participants in the FG discussions, 11 participants (73%) discussed this important topic and agreed with each other as they spoke about their own experiences in administering care for their children.

The following are responses from participants in the study.

Participant # 19 (FG#1): "My understanding is being able to take care of the child physically, mentally, and socially (child's well-being). Being able to talk with your children when they have challenges. Take them for walks, be able to interact with your children regarding their experiences at school, helping them with their homework."

Participant # 23 (FG#2): "Knowing how to deal with your kids' highs and lows is important. There are times when kids are moody, and you don't know what is affecting them. So, we need to find a way to understand what is going on in their lives. Instead of jumping to conclusions, let us sit them down and talk with them. Being patient is also important."

Participant # 27 (FG#3): "Things you should do as a parent. A mother's intuition. You should be able to know your child even though they cannot speak. As a parent, you should know what they want."

Theme 7: Giving love and affection

This theme emerged from the response to question 5. What are the most essential skills young single parents need to help them become more confident as parents? The family structure represents the operational rules that govern the way family members interact with each other (UKessays 2015b). Focused attention means giving a child full, undivided attention in such a way that the child feels without a doubt completely loved (Campbell, 2015). This attention makes the child feel like the most important person in the world in his or her parents' eyes. Table 21 shows responses out of fifteen participants in the FG discussions, where 5 participants (33%) believed and expressed that giving love and affection is one of the most essential skills young single parents need to help them become more confident as parents. An equal number (33%) indicated that spending quality time with their children was a factor in helping single parents become more confident as parents.

Table 21

Most Essential Skills Young Single Parents Need to Help Them Become More Confident as Parents.

Most essential skills young single parents need to help them become more confident as parents	Number of responses	%
Giving love and affection	5	33%
Spending quality time with your children	5	33%
Total Participants	15	100%

The following are responses from participants in the study.

Participant # 26 (FG#2): "Being sensitive to the needs of your children. For example, try to understand what they need when they are crying and learn how to make them feel happy and comfortable."

Participant # 28 (FG#3): "Watching over and caring for your children."

Participant # 29 (FG#3): "Giving love and attention."

Theme 8: Spending quality time with your children

This theme emerged from the response to question 5. What are the most essential skills young single parents need to help them become more confident as parents? The study findings revealed that of the 15 participants in the FG discussions, 5 participants (33%) felt that spending quality time with their children is an essential skill that young single parents need. The following are some of the responses in the study.

Participant # 25 (FG#2): "Spending quality time with your children will develop a bond between you and them. And it will also encourage you to continue taking care of them."

Participant# 30 (FG# 3): "You have to lay down the rules in your home and be there to enforce them."

Participant # 33 (FG# 3): "Knowing your child. Being able to determine what to do and when to do it."

Theme 9: The need for community and government support

This theme emerged from the response to question 6. What can society do to address the challenges of young single-parent families? The participants are of the view that the community and the government have a pivotal role in helping young single-parent families. Of the 15 participants in the FG discussions, 13 participants (87%) highlighted several ways the community and government can assist young single-parent families. The following are some of the responses.

> **Participant # 20 (FG#1):** "Government support can provide classes free of cost for young single parents who are school dropouts."
>
> **Participant # 19 (FG#1):** "The NGOs, government, and religious organizations can partner with each other and roll out empowerment programs for young single parents in their role as parents. For example, the community center can be used to provide skill-based training and support in cash and kind. Also helping them to link with organizations and entities according to their training for employment."
>
> **Participant # 26 (FG#2):** "They can provide counselors to help us with the understanding of parenting."
>
> **Participant # 30 (FG#3):** "Help with school supplies for the children."

Theme 10: The collaboration of healthcare workers, social workers, and religious leaders

This theme emerged from the response to question 7. Who do you think are the main people and institutions that can address the issues of single-parent families? The study revealed that of the 15 participants, 8 (53%) shared their desire to see the collaboration of the healthcare workers, social workers, and religious leaders of the 'C' Field for the well-being of young single parents in this area. Participants expressed the following views.

> **Participant # 21 (FG#1):** "Religious leaders and social workers can visit the community and give encouragement to young single parents and their children."

> **Participant # 23 (FG#2):** "The church is a good example because the church is a community of people and they will be able to help the young mothers by teaching them how to raise their children."

Theme 11: Being a role model

This theme emerged from the response to question 8. What can you do to improve your parenting skills? The study findings reported that of the 15 participants in the FG discussions, 7 participants (47%) are determined to become role models as it relates to improving their parenting skills. The following are some responses to the study.

Participant # 21 (FG#1): "Be more open to your children. For example, show more concern for them. Your children can trust you to talk to you about anything."

Participant # 26 (FG#2): "Becoming a good role model. Model good behavior to my children so that they can observe and practice the same."

Theme 12: Mentorship

This theme emerged from the response to question 9. What can be done to develop the practical abilities of young single parents in their parenting? The study revealed that of the fifteen participants in the FG discussions, 8 participants (53%) see mentorship as a major intervention in helping young single parents develop their practical abilities in parenting. Participants expressed the following views.

Participant # 21 (FG#1): "Develop computer skills to teach your children how to use the computer."

Participant # 25 (FG#2): "Help in boosting my children's self-esteem. For example, give them rewards and compliment them when they do well."

Participant # 27 (FG#3): "Nurses can have a 30-minute seminar with mothers when they have clinic visits on the do's and don'ts of parenting. For example, how to bathe a baby, how to feed a baby, and how to burp a baby."

Convergence of the Main Themes Emerging from the Interviews and Focus Group Discussions

This section highlights some of the observations of similar themes in the individual interviews and the focus group discussions. Figure 3 highlights the trends discussed following, with data points closest to the outer border being representative of those themes with the highest responses.

Figure 3.
Similar Themes Emerged from the Interviews and Focus Group Discussions.

Similar themes emerging from interviews and focused groups

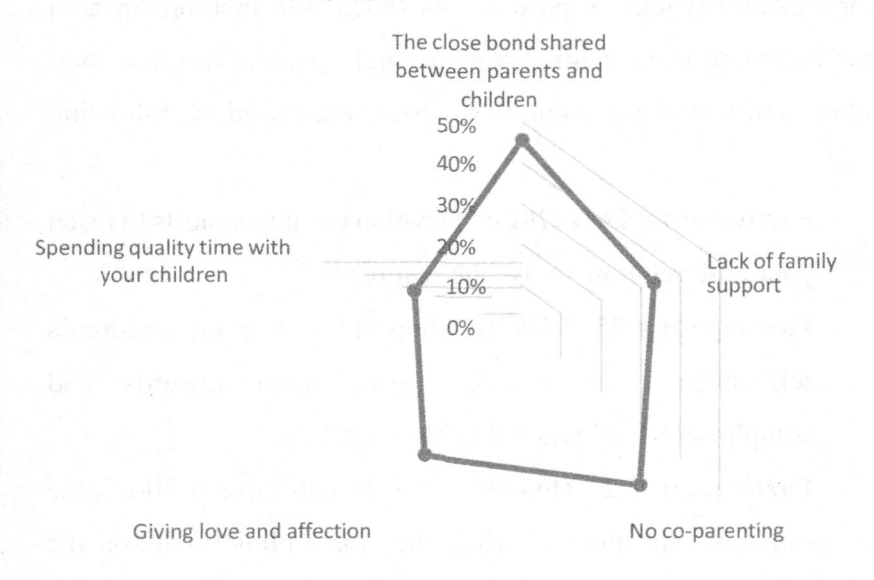

- The close bond shared between parents and children
- Spending quality time with your children
- Lack of family support
- Giving love and affection
- No co-parenting

(Scale: 0% – 50%)

The close bond shared between parents and children

Based on the responses to question 1 of the individual interviews and the focus group discussions,15 parents stated the close bond shared between themselves and their children, gives them joy and happiness in parenting. The participants agreed that this close bond creates and strengthens an attachment in the relationship and propels them to be determined not to give up on their children. This finding is supported by B.F. Skinner Operant Theory. McLeod, (2018) states "Through operant conditioning behavior which is reinforced(rewarded) will likely be repeated" (p. 1).

Lack of family support

Based on the responses to question 2 of the individual interviews and focus group discussions,11 parents stressed the need for family support in their daily child-raising efforts. Their inexperience in parenting has caused much mental and emotional stress on their total well-being.

No co-parenting

Based on the responses to question 3 of the individual interviews and the focus group discussions, 16 parents shared their regret about the other parent not playing a role in their children's growth and development. The need for both parents in a child's life is paramount and central to the necessary interactions of parent/child relationship and development. Clarke (1999) opined "The failure of the paternal relationship and the excessive reliance on the mother has its effect upon the young man when he grows up" (p. 123). Further, in a case study of single-parent families, Martin Beckford (as cited in UK Essays, 2015) submits,

> Children from broken homes are almost five times more likely to develop emotional problems than those living with both parents, a report has found. The report said: The odds of developing an emotional disorder were increased for children where there had been a change in the number of parents between surveys, from two parents to one parent, compared with children and young people in families that had two parents at both times. The report's author, Nina Parry-Langdon, said: "If children belong to more clubs, it may offer some protection against getting a disorder in the future. (p. 1)

Therefore, the absence of one parent, particularly the father, has caused some amount of deficiency in the day-to-day operational rules that are needed to guide their children to a stable future.

Giving love and affection

Based on the responses to question 5 of the individual interviews and the focus group discussions, 13 parents believed that giving love and affection to their children is one of the critical parenting skills needed to empower young single parents in their role as parents and helps to shape a child's happiness for life. Campbell (2015) highlights this link stating that "Unconditional love is a guiding light in child rearing" (p. 35).

Spending quality time with your children

Based on the responses to question 5 of the individual interviews and the focus group discussions,10 parents, viewed spending time with their children as another critical parenting skill needed for the empowerment of both parents and children. The participants believed that this parenting skill is apt in facilitating competent parenting among young single parents in 'C' Field Sophia, Georgetown, Guyana.

Answering the Primary Research Question

The primary research question was What can be done to facilitate competent parenting among single parents in "C" Field Sophia, Georgetown, Guyana? This question is addressed from two levels. The first is from the parental level and the second is from the community/societal level.

From the Parental Level

The study found that three similar themes emerged from the interviews and focus group discussions. The close bond shared between parents and children (45%), giving love and affection (39%), and spending quality time with your children (30%). These items represent the critical areas of parenting skills needed to facilitate competent parenting among young single parents in 'C' Field Sophia, Georgetown, Guyana.

It is against this backdrop that I believe single parents have the responsibility to constantly practice these parenting skills. Given time, and the consistent practice of these essential parenting skills, their practical abilities in parenting will improve. Parenting skills are important in positively influencing a child's life and development. Learning parenting skills have impacted positively thus increasing their knowledge and practice in their role of nurturing and caring for their children. Therefore, with this competence, the best practices are repeated to facilitate competent parenting and empower them in their role as parents.

From the community/societal level

The study found that the community of 'C' Field Sophia, Georgetown, Guyana, has a pivotal role to play in facilitating competent parenting. Eighty-seven percent of the participants in the focus group discussions believe there is a need for support. The following are some of the suggestions made by participants.

> **Participant # 20 (FG#1):** "Support groups can be created from the community including religious groups, non-governmental organizations, and the business community to give encouragement and counseling, a skills training

program is needed to give young single parents an opportunity to discover what they are good at, and religious organizations can sponsor a child or two to attend school."

Participant # 23 (FG#2): "Society can organize courses such as catering, hair and nails, nursing, and life skills so that young single parents can acquire a skill to better take care of their children."

Success story: "For me, even though I had my kids so early I completed school with CXC. As they got big, I went, and I did nursing, and presently I'm a private nurse. I'm able to take care of them with or without their father. I have also inspired my son who wants to be a Police Officer and my daughter who wants to be a nurse when they are older. Even though I made a mistake in the beginning I was able to correct it."

Participant # 33 (FG#3): "Reach out and help by showing us how to raise the children. Give counsel and teach life skills."

Counseling is needed in the following areas: 1) How to improve your self-esteem; 2) How to deal with anxiety; and 3) How to deal with anger. Participants are of the view that if society can provide help in these areas in their personal lives, it can mitigate much of the stress they experience. As a result, they will be able to focus on competent parenting. The study also found that mentorship is very important in facilitating competent parenting among young single parents in 'C' Field Sophia, Georgetown Guyana.

Answering the Supporting Research Questions

The first supporting research question was What skills do young single parents think they need to be parents? The study found that giving love and affection, providing a safe and secure environment, exercising patience, how to discipline their child, spending quality time with their children, and the ability to administer care for their children are all skills needed by young single parents to become parents.

The second supporting research question was What challenges are being faced by young single parents in their role as parents? The following challenges were revealed from the individual interviews and focus group discussions conducted.

1. meeting the daily needs of the children
2. lack of parental skills
3. lack of family support

The study also found that the reason given for the challenges is the fact that there is no co-parenting. Managing our spending and prioritizing our well-being were two experiences participants expressed that can help themselves and other young single parents in raising their children.

The third supporting question was What are some of the strategies to facilitate the parenting skills of young single-parent families? The study found that the participants expressed the strategies to facilitate parenting skills from two perspectives, individual and community.

From an individual perspective

The study found that the participants expressed a strong desire to take responsibility for improving their parenting skills. The following strategies were recommended by the participants.

1. improve their communication skills.
2. practice multitasking
3. have a "can do" attitude.
4. ask for help.
5. celebrate the achievements in parenting.
6. being a role model

From a community perspective

The study also found that participants expressed the view that the community of 'C' Field Sophia has a vital role in facilitating the improvement of their parenting skills. Participants recommended the strategy of collaboration among healthcare workers, social workers, and religious leaders in the community. I believe this broad base approach recommended by the participants augers well for them and is a display of their determination to be empowered in their role as parents. One participant expressed the following view.

> **Participant # 27 (FG#3)**: "Nurses can have a 30-minute seminar with mothers when they have clinic visits on the do's and don'ts of parenting. For example, how to bathe a baby, how to feed a baby, and how to burp a baby."

Results of the Transformational Strategy

Description

The objectives of the seminar were to inspire young single parents to engage in the process of personal growth and development that will transform their lives and to provide a safe space for parents to share their experiences and co-create dreams for their families. Participants were reminded of the empowerment seminar one week before its implementation, via telephone calls and WhatsApp messages. The seminar was divided into two sessions. The first session was in the form of a PowerPoint presentation with a duration of one hour, and the second session was in the form of an activity for the participants with a duration of two hours.

The one-day empowerment seminar on personal growth and development was implemented based on the pressing need discovered in the study. Participants admitted that the major responsibility of parenting has caused them to place their personal growth and development on hold. Nonetheless, participants think that they need to find a way to focus on at least one area of personal growth and development in the near future. Further, they are of the view that for them to empower their children, they need to be empowered also. This transformation strategy has answered a personal question about participants finding a way to pursue their personal goals and ideas of how to improve their own lives. Linthicum (2003) articulated "The way to enable people to 'do for themselves' is by enabling them to work together to empower each other, not by developing a program that only strengthens their dependency" (p. 151). This empowerment seminar was implemented on Saturday, October 2022, at The First Assembly of God- Judah located in 'C' Field Sophia, Georgetown, Guyana. This empowerment seminar brought together 12 participants in the research.

Using the appreciative inquiry 4-D cycle approach, each participant was involved in an activity to complete a questionnaire. The following are the responses under the 4-D cycle.

DISCOVER- Identify one area of your life for personal growth and development. Figure 4 shows that of the 12 participants, 4 participants (33%) stated a desire to become an entrepreneur, and 8 participants (67%) stated pursuing higher education.

Figure 4

Responses from 'Discover' Activity - Identify one area of your life for personal growth and development

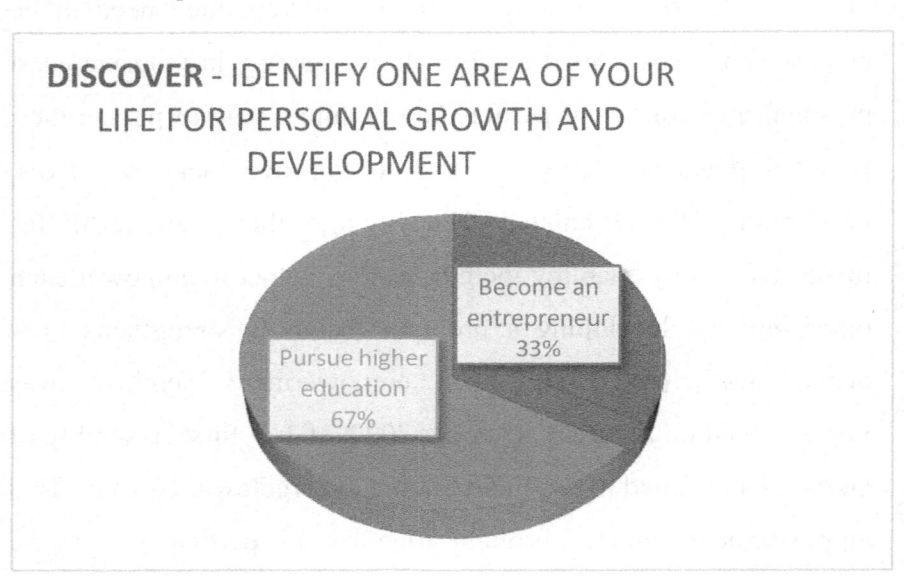

DISCOVER - IDENTIFY ONE AREA OF YOUR LIFE FOR PERSONAL GROWTH AND DEVELOPMENT

- Pursue higher education 67%
- Become an entrepreneur 33%

DREAM- Identify an institution you would like to attend to achieve the goal of personal growth and development. Figure 5 shows that of the 12 participants, 5 participants (42%) listed Carnegie School of Home Economics, 2 participants (17%) Government Technical Institute, 2 participants (17%) Texila University (Guyana), while 1 participant (8%) each indicated The Business School, School of Nursing, and The University of Guyana.

Table 22

Responses from 'Dream' Activity - Identify an institution you would like to attend to achieve the goal of personal growth and development

DREAM-Institution you would like to attend	Responses	%
Carnegie School of Home Economics	5	42%
Government Technical Institute	2	17%
Texila University	2	17%
The Business School	1	8%
School of Nursing	1	8%
The University of Guyana	1	8%

DESIGN – Write a short-term plan to achieve the goal of personal growth and development. All 12 participants agreed to enquire about the requirements for enrollment, contact the institutions (via phone or email), apply to the institutions, and enroll for the specific discipline of interest.

DESTINY – Figure 5 shows that of the 12 participants, 5 participants (42%) listed successful entrepreneurs, while 3 participants (25%) listed pursuing higher education overseas. Similarly, one participant (8%) listed qualifying as an immigration officer, working as a certified machinist, a certified welder, and a registered nurse as their desired destiny over the next three years.

Figure 5

Responses from 'Destiny' Activity - How do you see yourself in the next 1 to 3 years?

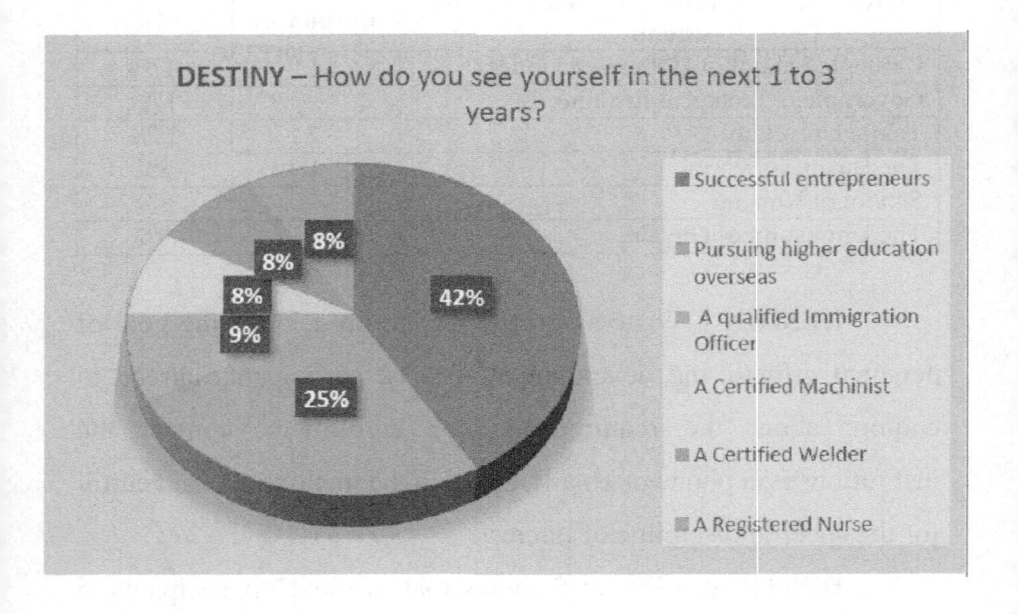

DESTINY – How do you see yourself in the next 1 to 3 years?

- Successful entrepreneurs: 42%
- Pursuing higher education overseas: 25%
- A qualified Immigration Officer: 9%
- A Certified Machinist: 8%
- A Certified Welder: 8%
- A Registered Nurse: 8%

Post–Seminar Feedback

The following are some of the responses from a post-seminar interview of participants at the end of the seminar.

Question 1: What impacted you the most in this seminar?

Participant # 27: "The advice we got on how to deal with anger and more so personal growth and development. I think that is one of the biggest things that touched me because I'm now learning how to control my anger, and how to deal with problems as a mother."

Participant # 19: "I feel happy to know that we are getting help."

Participant # 20: "For me knowing that I will go from this point on and start achieving the goals that I have set out today. And I am excited to see it take off."

Participant # 11: "The diagram with the 4-D cycle touched me the most."

Participant # 17: "The importance of growth and development. I am at that stage in my life right now. So, I'm glad that I came to get more ideas about the importance of growth and development."

Question 2: What are some of the changes you experienced being a part of this seminar?

Participant # 27: "Mostly my mindset. I have a mindset to further my studies, going after what I wanted to do before having the child."

Participant # 19: "A mindset change. I just need to go a little more, and I will achieve my goals."

Participant # 20: "I was encouraged to know that I'm not the only one going through certain things. Coming together today has opened my eyes that there are other mothers with the same challenges, working now to be a better version of ourselves."

Participant # 11: "Some of the changes are, how to control my emotions. I have a problem controlling my anger. Today I have learned how to deal with that."

Participant # 17: "I've learned that life comes with different changes and you have to learn how to deal with them."

Question 3: What will you do differently from today?

Participant # 27: "From today I will stop doubting myself because all your life you are hearing you can't do this; you can't do that. I can have a child, pursue my studies, and have a career. So, I'm going to go after that."

Participant # 19: "I know I will go forward and put everything into practice that I set out to do. My goals. And I will start working toward them."

Participant # 11: "Be nice to others and always have a plan for your life."

Participant # 17: "I will continue to improve in my growth and development."

Question 4: What was your overall impression of this seminar?

Participant # 27: "It was a great seminar, and it was well-needed in our community. We needed to hear the things that were taught in the seminar. It is something that should be done more often. That support, that push to say you can do it, you can further your studies, you can open that business. Sometimes we just need that push and that help."

Participant # 19: "It was empowering, and I felt good that somebody listened and heard me."

Participant # 20: "I think it was a beautiful seminar. Not often we would get people coming to just listen to us and actually help us. I just want to say thank you and it was just beautiful."

Participant # 11: "It was extremely helpful. We learned something new."

Participant # 17: "The seminar was particularly good. I am glad that I came and hope to see many more. I wish to pass these messages on to other young women so that they can learn to have confidence in themselves. There are many young mothers and individuals who are glad to see that someone is reaching out to them. Some people tend to feel that no one cares and to know that someone reaching out to you at least they can have a little confidence. So, I am happy."

Participants have expressed a deep desire to embark on the trajectory of implementing their action plan to achieve their goals of personal growth and development. Participants have also pledged to work feverishly in meeting those requirements as part of the process of realizing their goals on time. This decision will aid in the process of transformation and empowerment of the participants. Smith (as cited in Fikkert & Kapic, 2019) posited,

> To be human is to be for something, directed toward something, oriented toward something. To be human is to be on the move, pursuing something, after something. We are not just static containers for ideas; we are dynamic creatures directed toward some end. (p. 51)

Summary

The findings from this study confirm that single parents in 'C' Field Sophia Georgetown, Guyana, are experiencing challenges in parenting. Participants identified the reasons for the challenges they are facing and the possible strategies they can employ to mitigate those challenges. The data produced the perceptions, experiences, and understanding of the critical areas of parenting skills that are needed to empower young single parents in their role as parents. The data revealed that there are some main strategies to be fully embraced and implemented to facilitate competent parenting in their daily child-raising experiences and personal growth and development. The data also highlights the collaborative approach that is vital for parents, community leaders, and government officials to take in the rolling out of programs that will bring support and transformation in the lives of young single parents in 'C' Field Sophia Georgetown, Guyana, and further afield. Some of the Bakke Graduate University (2020) transformational leadership perspectives were critical interventions in the delivery of leadership and empowerment training.

CHAPTER 5
RECOMMENDING WORKABLE SOLUTIONS FOR SINGLE PARENTING SUCCESS

This chapter describes a brief interpretation of the results of the study. This description is a summary of the validity and trustworthiness of the project, its significance, and implications, the communication strategies discovered, and the replicability of the transformational model implemented. The chapter concludes with important recommendations for future action steps.

Interpretation of the Results

Patton (as cited in Sensing, 2011) defines *interpretation* as follows.

Interpretation is going beyond the descriptive data. Interpretation means attaching significance to what was found, making sense of findings, offering explanations, drawing conclusions, extrapolating lessons, making inferences, considering meanings, and otherwise imposing order on an unruly but surely patterned world. (p. 213)

The study results answered the research questions, and the main research question. What can be done to facilitate competent parenting among single parents in 'C' Field Sophia, Georgetown, Guyana?

The close bond shared between parents and children, giving love and affection, and spending quality time with their children were three key convergent themes revealed as critical areas of parenting skills to facilitate competent parenting among single parents in 'C' Field Sophia, Georgetown, Guyana. Therefore, the consistent practice of these three findings will give parents the confidence they need to become competent parents and demonstrate positive parenting. Parents must understand and practice the value of attachment, which helps the growing child to form bonds beyond his or her immediate circle of people to the wider community. The finding is supported by the attachment theory explained in Chapter 2, where Ali and Soomar (2019) comment on the fact that "Parents facilitate their children in each step of their life and love them unconditionally" (p. 1). Tomlinson (2022) proffers,

> Many parents are conscious of how bonding and attachment are vital for a child's well-being. Secure attachment is about attuning to your child's needs and responding appropriately. Securely attached children are more confident, have stronger and more positive relationships overall, are better at problem-solving, believe they can achieve, have a higher sense of self-worth, and are more resilient. (p. 1)

Li (2022) proffers,

Parents are attachment figures according to the Attachment Theory. A quality parent-child relationship is uniquely important to children since a child's sense of emotional security and psychological well-being is dependent on it. As a result, parental love has an unparalleled influence on a child's character, personality development, and outcomes. (p. 1)

Alvardo (n.d. as cited by Claire Roudabush, 2019) states, Quality time is time with your children and giving them your undivided attention doing tasks that they like to do. Spending quality time with your children does not have to be a huge undertaking, it can be as simple as taking a few minutes each day to spend together without distractions. (p. 1)

The supporting research questions were as follows.

What skills do young single parents think they need to be parents?

It is important to note that the following themes revealed some of the necessary skills young single parents think they need to be parents.

1. providing a safe and secure environment for your children
2. exercising patience
3. how to discipline your child
4. how to manage your spending

5. prioritizing your well-being
6. becoming a parent
7. the ability to administer care for your children

In retrospect, some participants shared the fact that they were not prepared mentally, emotionally, and physically for the important responsibility of parenting. Therefore, they encountered several pitfalls in their trial-and-error attempts at parenting. However, they believe that experience teaches wisdom and hope that expressing the necessity of these skills, can foster better parenting for themselves, other young single parents, and potential parents. In a similar research, Bhat and Patil (2019) found that "Single parenting is a social sacrifice and unpleasant test of stamina in one's life for bringing up the child" (p. 161). Taking the role of parenting step-by-step and making the best of everyday moments is a "can do" attitude that will encourage positive parenting and will help parents feel less stressed and anxious to give their children what they need to grow and develop well.

What challenges are being faced by young single parents in their role as parents?

This supporting research question was addressed from three perspectives.

1. challenges faced
   - meeting the daily needs of my children

- lack of parenting skills
- lack of family support
2. reasons for the challenges
    - no co-parenting
3. addressing the challenges
    - overcoming financial burdens
    - balancing personal development and parenting

The study findings show that young single parents face challenges in their parenting, giving the reason for the challenges faced and how to address these challenges. These three perspectives give an understanding of the severity of the challenges and ongoing efforts that are being made to address and overcome these challenges.

Participants are of the view that the genesis of these challenges stems from the fact that there is no co-parenting in raising their children. In Minuchin's family structure theory, Cherry (2021) "addresses how much members of the family relate to one another. The goal is to improve communication and relationships to create positive changes for both individual family members and the family unit as a whole" (p. 2). Participants have expressed that the lack of family support and no co-parenting have severely stymied the actualization of this goal in their families. Therefore, participants have resolved to apply the principles of reflective leadership, where parents will reflect on the reality and the true meaning of being a parent and intentionally work on bringing a balance among personal development, parenting, and the building of a quality relationship with their children.

What are some of the strategies to facilitate the parenting skills of young single-parent families?

The following themes were revealed in the study as strategies to facilitate parenting skills of young single-parent families in 'C' Field Sophia Georgetown, Guyana. The careful co-creation of this action plan by the participants fostered momentum for parents to work together and emphasized the destiny phase of the appreciative inquiry approach 4 D cycle. Participants were of the view that this approach provided an opportunity for a more effective form of empowering young single parents in their role as parents and creating the positive change they want to see in the lives of their children. Cooperrider et al. (2008) corroborate when they say,

> The *Destiny* phase delivers new images of the future and is sustained by nurturing a collective sense of purpose and movement. It is a time of continuous learning, adjustment, and improvisation (like a jazz group)- all in the service of shared ideals. The momentum and potential for innovation and implementation are extremely high. By this stage in the process, because of the shared positive image of the future,

everyone is invited to align his or her interactions in cocreating the future. (p. 46)

These are the following themes:

1. improving communication skills
2. multitasking
3. have a "can do" attitude
4. know your limitations
5. ask for help
6. celebrate the achievements in your parenting
7. the need for community and government support
8. the collaboration of healthcare workers, social workers, and religious leaders
9. being a role model
10. mentorship

Transformational Leadership Perspectives Explained

One of the signal interventions in the empowerment seminar was the tag team presentation of the concepts of shalom leadership and reflective leadership by myself and Mr. Wesley Adams - a qualified social worker who assisted me in the execution of the seminar. The shalom leadership concepts enumerated were "The leader pursues reconciling relationships between people, people and God, people and their environment, and people and themselves. The leader works towards the well-being, abundance, and wholeness of the community, as well as individuals" (Bakke Graduate University, 2020). The reflective leadership concepts enumerated were living in the reality of being a parent, reflecting on its meaning, catalyzing their children with courage, and examples to make meaning in their own lives. Participants noted that the application of these concepts is key to bringing the nexus between their families and the community in the transformation process. Participants also recommended that this intervention be launched as a pilot program in the community of 'C' Field Sophia and further afield. The practical approach emboldened participants to ask questions, seek clarification, and share their views on these leadership perspectives that they were hearing for the first time.

The Validity and Trustworthiness of the Study

Merriam and Tisdell (2016) state "Ensuring validity and reliability in qualitative research involves conducting the investigation in an ethical manner" (p. 237). Based on this idea, the validity of my data collection was discussed in Chapter 3. I believe by using the triangulation of individual interviews and focus group discussions, there was an establishment of convergent themes, views, and perceptions. The empowerment seminar itself was very effective since the content brought out one area for growth and development in the lives of the participants and placed them on a trajectory to achieve those goals of growth and development.

Significance and Implications

One lesson I learned from this study is for transformational leadership to be effective, people must be taught these leadership principles. People need to be told that they are valuable, and loved, and they can make a positive change in their lives. I have also learned that some of the young single-parent fathers do not want to express their views on the notion of the critical areas of parenting skills needed to empower young single parents in their role as parents. Although it was a purposive study, I expected that more single-parent fathers would have responded. I also noted that the stakeholders of the community of 'C' Field Sophia, Georgetown, including health care workers, nongovernmental organizations (NGOs), religious leaders, and family members of participants in this study have a pivotal role to play in facilitating competent parenting among young single parents. Under the current circumstances, participants are finding it difficult to raise the next generation. However, there is hope, given the fact that I took the time to conduct this study, and participants now have a paradigm shift in the way they see themselves and the role they play in the growth and development of their children. The presence of fathers and father figures in the home is needed in the process of rearing and caring for children growing up in adverse conditions. Finally, I learned that building strong relationships at the parental level, the family level, and the community level can help mitigate some of the major challenges faced by young single mothers in their daily child-raising experiences.

Communication Strategies Discovered

An aspect of this study was concerned with effectively communicating with leaders of some of the key institutions such as the 'C' Field Health Center, the 'C' Field Nursery School, the Deliverance Assembly of God Church, and the First Assembly of God Church -Judah. I discovered that the effective communication strategy and power of networking were instrumental in these leaders doing the groundwork to make the connection with myself and the participants in the study. The use of texting and WhatsApp messages proved to be less costly in finalizing arrangements with participants before the face-to-face interviews and focus group discussions. My listening ability to be attentive and the interpretation of body language were nonverbal skills developed in the process of understanding the participants' concerns.

Replicability of the Transformational Model Implemented

The model of an empowerment seminar used as the vehicle for a transformational strategy was highly effective and interactive. It fostered an opportunity for participants who are experiencing similar challenges in parenting to share their experiences and learn how to overcome and focus on positive parenting and brought a sense of hope among the participants. According to Greenleaf (1991), "Hope, it seems to me, is absolutely essential to both sanity and wholeness in life" (p. 3). The key takeaways follow.

1. Young single parents left the seminar with a mindset change, a buy-in, and tools to focus on how to achieve their goals of personal growth and development.
2. Young single parents empathized with each other, given the fact that they are not alone in their trials and triumphs in parenting.
3. Young single parents felt and expressed that someone cared about their well-being and was willing to focus on solutions.
4. A momentum of networking and collaboration has started among young single parents, and with the intervention of building relationships, there is hope in achieving their goals.
5. Young single parents left the seminar with the strategy of "each one tell one" to share the knowledge gained with other single parents in the community and further afield.

The use of a PowerPoint presentation added to the interest of the discussion since participants interacted with the information on each slide and asked questions to clarify their understanding of the concepts shared. This intervention was practical and meaningful and can be replicated in communities around Guyana and the Caribbean because of the need for empowerment of young single parents in their role as parents.

Recommendations

Based on the findings of this study and the methodology I employed, I recommend the following.

1. **Investigation** - Further studies should be conducted to investigate the reasons for no co-parenting by some of the young single-parent fathers in 'C' Field Sophia, Georgetown, Guyana.

2. **National Mentorship Programs** – A consultation should be done with the Gender Affairs Bureau of the Ministry of Human Services and Social Security to formulate an appropriate comprehensive mentorship program for young single parents in 'C' Field Sophia Georgetown, Guyana.

3. **Collaborative Counseling** – As distinct from the mentorship program, a consultation with the Gender Affairs Bureau of the Ministry of Human Services and Social Protection could organize appropriate relationship counseling sessions to address matters of low self-esteem, anger management, emotional healing,

and mental health well-being among young single parents in 'C' Field Sophia Georgetown, Guyana.

4. **Deliver Shalom Leadership training** - A consultation with the institutions that granted the permission to conduct the study in the community to organize training sessions for the introduction and implementation of the principles of shalom leadership and reflective leadership would be helpful.

5. **Leverage data for decision making** - Government entities such as the Ministry of Human Services and Social Protection could use data from this study to fund programs that will bring aid and assistance in the areas of need identified.

6. **Adapt international response for community solutions** - Nongovernmental organizations such as the United Nations International Children's Emergency Fund, United Nations Development Programme, and the United Nations High Commissioner for Refugees could use the data to fund programs that will bring relief to people based on the problems they are experiencing in the community.

7. **Leverage Church Ministry for Community Service** - Church ministry activities adapted to target the needs of

this specific population (single parent) in communities; family and marriage department, women's ministry, men's ministry, and youth ministry activities and messages tailored to address single parent needs rather than generalized engagement on topics such as parenting, financial management, and self-empowerment.

Conclusion

The problem of young single parents in 'C' Field Sophia Georgetown, Guyana, experiencing challenges in parenting does exist. The resolution to this problem is to take a collaborative approach as parents, community leaders, and leaders of government and nongovernmental organizations to address the problem at its core. This approach will address topics such as organized relationship counseling to address issues of low self-esteem, mental health well-being, anger management, a structured mentorship program and a pilot training program in shalom leadership and reflective leadership.

Participants in the study have shown a high level of commitment and dedication in fulfilling their part to facilitate competent parenting and empowerment in their role as parents. The implementation of this approach will take further consultation with the other stakeholders who granted permission to conduct the study in 'C' Field Sophia, Georgetown, Guyana, and the Ministry of Human Services and Social Protection to decipher the appropriate methodologies to be used for its implementation.

I have taken a people-oriented and values-oriented approach to writing this book. I am happy to report that the process of transformation has begun. Our communities will heal when single-parent households are empowered differently. Transformation is about people. Once they can see it, they will pursue it, experience it and own it.

REFERENCE LIST

Acting Colleges. (2022). *What is a limitation of operant conditioning?* https://actingcollegeses.com/library/acting-questions/read/16690-what-is-a-limitation-of-operant-conditioning

Ainsworth, M., Bowlby, J. (1991). The origins of attachment theory: John Bowlby and Mary Ainsworth Inge Bretherton. *Psychology.* https://www.psychology.sunysb.edu/attachment/online/inge_origins.pdf

Applebury, G. (2022). *Types of family therapy: Pros & cons of common techniques.* https://family.lovetoknow.com/about-family-values/types-family-therapies-choose-from

Ali, S., & Soomar, M. (2019). Single parenting: Understanding reasons and consequences. *JOJ Nursing & Health Care, 10*(2), 1- 3.DOI:10.19080/JOJNHC.2019.10.555781 https://juniperpublishers.com/jojnhc/JOJNHC.MS.ID.555781.php

Bakke Graduate University. (2020). *Transformational leadership perspectives.* https://bgu.edu/programs/transformational-leadership-perspectives

Better Health Channel. (2022). Single parenting: Single parenting and dual parenting. *Betterhealth*. https://www.betterhealth.vic.gov.au/health/healthyliving/single-parenting

Bhat, N. A., & Patil, R.R. (2019). Single parenthood families and their impact on children in India. *Delhi Psychiatry Journal, 22*(1), 160-164. https://researchgate.net/profile/Nabat-Arfi/publication/344904774_Parental_Handling_Measures_Among_Physically_Challenged_children/links/5f985b5592851c14bced2de0/

Bushe, G. (2021). *Appreciative inquiry: Theory and critique*. https://www.researchgate.net/publication/303265521

Campbell, D.R. (2015). *How to really love your child* (2nd ed). David C. Cook.

Cherry, K. (2020). Transformational leadership: A closer look at the effects of transformational leadership. *Verywell Mind*. https://www.verywellmind.com/what-is-transformational-leadership-2795313

Cherry, K. (2021). Structural family therapy: Definition, techniques, and efficacy. *Verywell Mind*.

https://www.verywellmind.com/what-is-structural-family-theraphy-5193068

Cherry, K. (2022). What is attachment theory? The importance of early emotional bonds. *Verywell Mind.* https://www.verywellmind.com/what-is-attachment-theory-2795337

Cherry, K. (2023). Operant conditioning: What it is, how it works, and examples. *Verywell Mind.* https://www.verywellmind.com/operant-conditioning-a2794863

Clarke, E. (1999). *My mother who fathered me: A study of the families in three selected communities of Jamaica.* The Press University of The West Indies.

Clothed with Dignity. (2020). 3 *Incredible single moms in the Bible.* https://clothedwithdignityco.com/single-moms-bible/

Cook, J. (2021). Single parent definition and effects. *Study.* https://study.com/learn/lesson/single-parent-definition-effects.html

Cooperrider, D., Whitney, D., & Stavros, J. (2008). *The appreciative inquiry handbook: For leaders of change* (2nd ed). Crown Custom Publishing, Inc.

Cordeiro, P. (2022). *Family structure and education: Spotlight on single mother households in Trinidad and Tobago.* Global Ed Leadership. https://globaledleadership.org/2022/06/13/family-structure-and-education-spotlight-on-single-mother-households-in-trinidad-and-tobago

Cresswell, J.W., & Cresswell, J.D. (2018). *Research design: Qualitative, quantitative, and mixed methods approach* (5th ed.). Sage Publications Inc.

Corbett, S., & Fikkert, B. *When helping hurts: How to alleviate poverty without hurting the poor and yourself.* Moody Publishers.

Encyclopaedia Britannica. (2015). *Britannica, the editors of encyclopaedia. "Georgetown"* https://www.britannica.com/place/Georgetown-Guyana

Fikkert, B., & Kapic, K. M. (2019). *Becoming whole: Why the opposite of poverty isn't the American dream.* Moody Publishers.

Got Questions. (2022). *What does the Bible say about single parents/parenting?* https://www.gotquestions.org/single-parenting.html

Goker, S., & Bozkus, K. (2017). *Reflective leadership: Learning to manage and lead human organizations.* https://cdn.intechopen.com/pdfs/52166.pdf

Greenleaf, R. (1991). *Servant leadership: A journey into the nature of legitimate power and greatness.* Paulist Press.

Guyana Population and Housing Census (2012). Bureau of Statistics Guyana.

Henry, P. (2017). Child neglect in Guyana Paulette Henry. *Better Care Network.* https://bettercarenetwork.org/sites/default/files/Child-Neglect-Research-Final-Report-pdf

Kiger, M.E., & Varpio, L. (2020). *Thematic analysis of qualitative data: AMEE guide No. 131.* Plymouth. https://www.plymouth.ac.uk/uploads/production/document/path/18/18247/Kiger_and_Varpio2020Thematic_analysis_of_qualitative_data_AMEE_Guide_No_131.pdf

Kramer, S. (2019). The U.S. has the world's highest rate of children living in single- parent households. https://www.pewresearch.org/fact-tank/2019/12/12/u-s-children-more-likely-than-children-in-other-countries-to-live-with-just-one-parent/

Ken, P. (2007). Children without parental care in the Caribbean systems of protection. *Better Care Network.* https://bettercarenetwork.org/sites/default/files/attachments/Children%20Without%20Parental%20Care%20in%20the%20Caribbean.pdf

Li, P. (2022). *How parental love helps a child succeed in life.* parenting for brain. https://www.parentingforbrain.com/parental-love/

Linthicum, R.L. (2003). *Transforming power: Biblical strategies for making a difference in your community.* InterVarsity Press.

Maddox. (2023). *What is Bowen theory, and how can it help families through challenges?* https://www.betterhelp.com/advice/therapy/what-is-bowen-family-systems-theory

Maramara, Z. (2018, July 11). Shalom leadership. *Christian Leadership Alliance.* https://christianleadershipalliance.org/blog/2018/07/11/shalom-leadership-by-zenet-maramara/

Mary, C. (2016). Definitions for parenting skills. *Definitions.* https://www.definitions.net/definition/parenting+skills

McLeod, S. (2023). Operant conditioning: What it is, how it works, and examples. *Simply Psychology*. https://simplypsychology.org/operant-conditioning.html

Merriam, S. B. (2009). *Qualitative research: A guide to design and implementation*. Jossey-Bass.

Merriam, S. B., & Tisdell, E. J. (2016). *Qualitative research: A guide to design and implementation* (4th ed). Jossey-Bass.

Nwobodo, R. (2021). Poverty and the challenges of parenting: Issues and prospects.

Nnadiebube Journal of Philosophy, 5(1), 65-81.

https://acjol.org/index.php/NJP/article/view/1387/1372

Oshi, S.N., Abel, W.D., Agu, C.F., Omeje, J.C., Smith, P.W., Ukwaja, K.N., Roomes, T.R., Meka, I.A., Weaver, S., Rae, T., Oshi, D.C. (2018). Single parent family structure as a predictor of alcohol use among secondary school students. Alcohol and tobacco use in the caribbean. *Asian Pac J Cancer Prev,19*,19-23.

http://journal.waocp.org/article_60399_cdfb5068a33dcd025923e11f5057803b.pdf

Parveen, H., & Showkat, N. (2017). *Validity, reliability, generalizability.*

https://www.researchgate.net/publication/319128421_Validity_Reliability_Generalizability

Parvez, H. (2021). PsychMechanics: A*ttachment theory (meaning & limitations)*. https://www.psychmechanics.com/understanding-attachment-theory/

Pfeiffer, S. (2021). Family systems. Reference module in neuroscience and bio behavioral psychology 2021. *Science Direct Journals & Books*. https://www.sciencedirect.com/topics/medicine-and-dentistry/family-systems-theory

Radford, D. (2021, June 11). UWI open campus, delta sigma theta partner to help single mothers. *The Gleaner*. https://jamaica-gleaner.com/article/news/20210611/uwi-open-campus-delta-sigma-theta-partner-help-single-mother

Regain Editorial Team. (2023). *Family systems theory: Definition & what is it?* regain. https://www.regain.us/advice/family-systems-theory-definition-what-is-it

Roudabush, C. (2019, April 19). *Why spending quality time with your children is important*. South Dakota State University. https://extension.sdstate.edu/why-spending-quality-time-your-children-important

Sensing, T. (2011). *Qualitative research: A multi-method approach to projects for doctor of ministry theses*. Wipf & Stock.

The Spaced-Out Scientist. (2017, July 18). *Single parents worldwide: Statistics and trends*. https://spacedoutscientist.com/2017/07/18/single-parents-worldwide-statistics-and-trends/

Stack, R.J. & Meredith, A. (2018). The impact of financial hardship on single parents. An exploration of the journey from social distress to seeking help. *Journal of family and economic issues, 39*(2), 233-42. https://link.springer.com/article/10.1007/s10834-017-9551-6

Swindoll, C. (1990). *You and your child: A biblical guide for nurturing confident children from infancy to independence*. Thomas Nelson, Inc.

Tomlinson, R. (2022, December 26). Bonding between parents and children at every social age. *Baby Chick*. https://www.baby-chick.com/bonding-between-parents-and-children-at-every-social-age/

UKessays, (2015a, January 1). *Case study of single parent families*. UK Essays.

https://www.ukessays.com/essay/sociology/case-study-of-single-parent-families-sociology-essay.php

Ukessays. (2015b, January 1). *Sociology- The structural theory of family structure.* UK Essays. https://www.ukessays.com/essay/sociolgy/the-structural-theory-of-family-structure-sociology-essay.php

The United Nations Sustainable Development Group. (2021). Lonely island no more: In the Caribbean helping women overcome discrimination and abuse. https://unsdg.un.org/latest/stories/lonely-island-no-more-caribbean-helping-women-overcome-discrimination-and-abuse

Van Eymeren, A., Barker, A., McCabe, B., Elisara, C. (2017). *Urban shalom & the cities we need.* Urban Shalom Publishing.

APPENDIX A
ONE-ON-ONE INTERVIEW QUESTIONS

1. What is the best part of being a single parent?
2. Describe some of the challenges you face as a single parent.
3. What causes some of the challenges faced by young single parents?
4. Give an example of a challenge you faced as a single parent and how you addressed it.
5. What are the most essential skills young single parents need?
6. If there is one experience you can share to help other young single parents in raising their children, what would it be and why?
7. What can you do to improve your parenting skills?
8. What can be done to make parenting easier for young single parents?
9. What recommendations will you give to help young single parents become more confident as parents?

APPENDIX B
FOCUS GROUP DISCUSSION QUESTIONS

1. Share some of your peak experiences or high points in your parenting.
2. What challenges do you face in your daily child-raising experiences?
3. What are some of the reasons for the challenges faced by young single parents?
4. What is your understanding of parenting skills?
5. What are the most essential skills young single parents need to help them become more confident as parents?
6. What can society do to address the challenges of young single-parent families?
7. Who do you think are the main people and institutions that can address issues of single-parent families?
8. What can you do to improve your parenting skills?
9. What can be done to develop the practical abilities of young single parents in their parenting?

APPENDIX C
HOLISTIC EMPOWERMENT PLAN

The questionnaires completed by participants in the empowerment seminar were completed in duplicate, and the follow-up process with participants is ongoing to monitor their progress in the implementation of the action plan for their personal growth and development and to supervise the rolling out of these action plans.

Van Eymeren et al. (2017) corroborated.

> Reflective mentors move beyond programs and activities and focus on their mentoring experience in a way that will allow them and their mentees to find meaning within the context of their relationship. Through reflection, mentors could arrive at the transformation in their lives and their mentees' lives. (p. 167)

To further build on the follow-up of my first cohort of participants in the empowerment seminar held, this study is intended to develop a broader mentorship program that leverages my transformational leadership journey to address the identified gaps in single parenting. The development of the mentorship program will include the following elements.

Objective of the Mentorship Program

The objective of the program is to empower young single parents to improve their parenting skills through mentorship, skills training, and a support network at the community and national levels.

Target Population

The initial target is to expand the number of young single parents being mentored from 33 persons to 100 persons located in the Sophia, Georgetown area. As the program grows, the target population will expand beyond Sophia, leveraging the different churches found in communities with an evident need.

Design of the Mentorship Program

The program will seek to address needs expressed during the research through a combination of training and mentorship sessions, coaching, informal engagements (e.g. movie or games night), networking with higher institutions of learning, and places of potential employment.

Each participant or cohort will be registered for one year, followed by an evaluation and graduation. The graduation is intended as a moment in time to celebrate the progress made by the participants as well as to measure the impact of the program. Marketing of the program will be done via social media, partner organizations, and organic marketing.

Delivery of the mentorship program will include monthly skills training, quarterly coaching, and semiannual informal meetings. Engagement with higher institutions of learning, potential employers, and other government services will be assessed quarterly. Further, all program activities will be conducted throughout one to three hours maximum.

Some specific areas for skills training and coaching will include role modeling, communications, financial management, caring for infants, computer skills, building self-esteem, anger management, bonding with children, the importance of love and affection in parenting, preparing for job interviews, entrepreneurship, and pathway to higher education. There will also be spiritual empowerment to encourage parents to find their purpose in Christ as well as affirming to them that Jesus cares for their children just as He does for a two-parent child.

To achieve success, it will be important to connect with volunteers, the church, the community, and national institutions as providers of some specific services offered under the mentorship program. It will be important to partner with other churches to achieve the target reach of 100 people. This model of partnering will also ensure growth in future years. There is also a role for national institutions to provide social workers for counseling when needed and even health care workers to coach single parents on caring for infants that may be incorporated during standard visits to the health center.

Resources Required

The success of the program will depend on securing venues for the activities, facilitators, marketing of the program, refreshments to be served, and out-of-pocket expenses that may sometimes be needed to sustain the participation of some single parents. Venues would be secured free of cost using church or community building, while facilitators will be asked to volunteer on a 3-monthly basis while others will be paid. The cost to fund a single monthly activity including facilitator fees, refreshments, training material, marketing, and incidentals is estimated at GYD 230,000 or USD 1,095. The cost per year is therefore GYD 2,760,000 or USD 13,140. These costs will be covered by inviting corporate sponsorship, accessing government grants, and applying to nongovernmental organizations such as the United Nations International Children's Emergency Fund, the United Nations Development Programme, and the United Nations High Commissioner for Refugees.

Evaluation of Impact

The program will be evaluated from a client and provider perspective. From the client's perspective, to request participants of the mentorship program to provide feedback after every session, either orally or in questionnaire format. From a provider perspective, a semiannual evaluation of the attendance, quality, and impact of the session on meeting the need.

Made in the USA
Middletown, DE
24 July 2024